THE FIGHT FOR INFLUENCE:
WHY THE UNITED STATES CANNOT WIN ANY REGIONAL WAR AGAINST RUSSIA OR CHINA USA-SOCIALISM OR CAPITALISM?

RUSSIAN MISSILES, CHINA WORLDWIDE POLITICAL EXPANSION, USA ECONOMIC LIMITATIONS AND STRENGTHS

USA PENTAGON, CHINESE PEOPLE'S CONGRESS, RUSSIAN KREMLIN

ISBN # 978-0-578-55284-2
COPYRIGHT WORLDWIDE RIGHTS PROTECTED
RALPH SCHULTZ
ALBUQUERQUE NEW MEXICO USA
MAY 31, 2019

BIOGRAPHY

I was born and lived on Chicago's South Side from 1947-1957 and then in Evergreen Park where I graduated from High School in 1965, a Chicago southwest suburb. Then I went to Northwestern University in Evanston, Illinois where I graduated in 1969 with a honors major in history and Russian Studies. I received a Master of Business degree in finance and economics in 1972. I worked for 35 years in the investment business as a corporate bond specialist and in equipment leasing and structured finance for international banks in Chicago including as a vice-president for Deutsche Bank, the leading bank in Germany. I switched to teaching in 2003 and worked at tribal colleges from 2005-2009 at the Pine Ridge Indian Reservation in South Dakota and the Navajo Reservation in Arizona. For the past nine years since 2009 I have taught economics at Central New Mexico Community College. In 1968 I went to Moscow Russia, the Soviet Union, to study Russian language and culture with a USA college group. I was a strategic intelligence analyst in the United States Army. I currently reside in New Mexico.

YOU WILL LEARN ABOUT:

Problems with USA foreign policy viewpoints about Russia and China and a possible military conflict outcome.

What it means that Russia and China are historically autocratic centrally controlled empires that have been invaded many times by foreign powers. There is no history of Western liberal democracy.

Some current critical issues about the USA economy today and how it affects you.

My background as a world class 800-meter runner and aspects about growing up in Chicago in 1947-65.

RALPH SCHULTZ   ECONOMICS PROFESSOR NEW MEXICO   USA Email: ralphschultz77@GMAIL.COM

RUSSIA 1968

Me and Russian schoolchildren and teacher outside Leningrad 1968: NOTE sandy ground near Finnish Gulf. So friendly and peaceful, America and the USSR.

TABLE of CONTENTS

THE STORY----SECTIONS

NOTE: I did my own editing which was a long arduous process. You will see imperfections and inconsistencies in spacing, picture placement, highlighting sentences, hyphens, some typos. Hey, I am imperfect and so are people and the world. I think the book works, is attractive, and very readable with many great photos. And I am honest about myself and my thoughts, beliefs. So read and enjoy! Learn. It took 3 ½ years to write this book and its two sister books, a total of 466 pages and 250 photographs. Another book recently published is about my life growing up in Chicago from 1947-1965 and my athletic career as an outstanding USA middle-distance runner. A third book to be published soon is about my time on the Lakota and Navajo Indian Reservations from 1996-2008

ACKNOWLEDGEMENTS

I would like to thank Merrillyn Sweet, my high school classmate, who voluntarily assisted me to put together the photographs, transcribe my oral recordings and helped with the computer, which I have to admit is difficult for me at times. Merrillyn and I met three years ago at a high school reunion, and we have become friends. She lives in the Chicago Metropolitan area in Riverside a beautiful suburb with many parks and trees and well maintained older classical homes. And two designed by Frank Lloyd Wright, the famous architect. Thank you Merrillyn.

And to Blaine, my 29-year-old son. Thank you for helping me managing photographs and getting it published and marketed on social media.

Kurt Tyler helped with technical issues. He is the author of two recent books, Diverse Career Paths, and another about racial relations.

And thank you to my Russian teachers; Mrs. Helen Sirel from Evergreen Park High School; Professor Irwin Weil from Northwestern University, world renown expert on Russian culture and society; Mrs. Youhn, Northwestern University; and my Russian teacher near Leningrad, Russia, the summer of 1968; and Professor David Joravsky, Russian history, Northwestern University

I speak a little Russian, but I would like to speak it more completely. Sometimes I practice and study. Ya Nechevo Nez Naiou—I know nothing, haha!

PREFACE

I wrote this book because I wanted to express my thoughts about ideas that matter to me that I want to express to many people. I have a lifelong wealth of wisdom and teach economics at a community college. I also traveled to Russia/Soviet Union in 1968. It made a major impression on me. I think athletes can and should speak out on issues that they think are important. The book is based upon extensive material I have read in many books, respected magazines and internet sites, and the mass media. It is not intended to be a scholarly work. I have synthesized information and drawn conclusions. I am a good thinker. It is about raising AWARENESS. The book is my take/viewpoint on critical world issues affecting the United States.

Some of you may still not understand why an athlete would make commentaries about world issues. Because it is who I am. Athletes are multifaceted and can offer their insights that will be respected and challenge another person's ideas and provide food for thought to consider and ponder. We need not always listen to experts, politicians, and news people.

I am NOT a national pundit and commentator that you see on national television news. I am an average person with an excellent education expressing insights that the American people must know, understand, and evaluate to challenge conventional ideas that are in the mass media and then make informed decisions.

So come along and share my journey and have a good read.

Ralph Schultz   May 31, 2019

NOTE: I started The Book in July 2015. Some of my political ideas preceded what is now commonly in the news. Namely, the US Deep State concept, athletes and celebrities as being outspoken on topics besides athletics, and the Russian viewpoint on foreign policy with the USA and NATO, what needs to be understood and done. And Cyberwarfare. The Putin-Trump summit in late July 2018 placed these topics and the Russian viewpoint in the national news media. This book is NOT about RussiaGate.

THE BOOK

This book is about the United States conflict of foreign policy with Russia and China which may result in a brief but violent regional conventional missile war. It presents the Russian and Chinese points of view, that are rarely discussed in the media. It also examines the conflict in Ukraine with emphasis on the Maidan and the violence in 2014 and suggests a solution to these issues. Today's characteristics and trends of the USA economy are also discussed and the economic Surge growth period of the 1950's. I believe that since I am a very successful American athlete and a former corporate banker it adds credibility to this book as it shows the viewpoint of an average well-educated informed American speaking to most Americans who might be disillusioned and questioning national elites and the media leading the population in the wrong direction.

I am dedicating this book to a kinder gentler world.

EARTH

WHY I WROTE THIS BOOK as an average person. I am not another national expert telling the American what to do and believe.

The first part of this book is a brief background summary from my prior book regarding my 10 years as an outstanding middle-distance runner and growing up in Chicago during 1947-65. It is primarily pictures. I include this background to present myself as an average American who was a great athlete and is willing to be bold to present America's so called enemies' (Russia and China) point of view to foreign policy and the West/USA. These viewpoints are rarely presented in the media.

I also comment on the USA economy, both strengths and weaknesses as an economics professor for the past 14 years after a career in corporate banking.

<u>**RUSSIA BEGINS ON PAGE 38 AND CHINA ON PAGE 98.**</u>

READERS NOTES:

WHAT DO YOU WANT TO LEARN FROM THIS BOOK?

DO YOU THINK RUSSIA AND CHINA MAY HAVE LEGITIMATE REASONS FOR THEIR FOREIGN POLICIES? PLEASE EXPLAIN

MY ACCOMPLISHMENTD IN TRACK

Living on the South Side of Chicago 1950's

MARCH 1969 CHICAGO TRIBUNE

Yes, I had quite a 10-year life as a star track athlete. Not one of the super best in the world, but close. Sixth ranked in the USA in high school (secondary school) in 1965 (1:51.9 800 meters). Third in the National Collegiate Athletic Association (NCAA) outdoor 880 in 1968 and All American. Big 10 Outdoor 880 Champion in 1967 and 1000 yard run Indoor Champion in 1968, 1969, Olympic tryout finalist 1968. Member of the 1970 and 1971 UCTC (University of Chicago Track Club coached by the highly regarded Ted Haydon) 2 Mile Relay teams that won the Indoor National Amateur Athletic Union (NAAU) Meet twice at Madison Square Garden in New York City on national television and many other first-place finishes. Tied the World Indoor 1000-yard record in 1969 held by Peter Snell of New Zealand (2:06). My best 800-meter time was 1:46.6 in 1969, 14th in the world, and tied with a Kenyan. I ran on a USA track team in Europe in 1970. I had the thrill to meet several all-time great athletes. When in high school I met and was interviewed by the great American sprinter Jesse Owens for a trip to the 1964 Olympic games as a good will ambassador to the Russian team. I was learning Russian in high school. I got to know Willie White, a FIVE-time woman Olympic long jumper at the University of Chicago Track Club meets, and on a USA track team sent to Europe to compete internationally. I had dinner with the Highland Park High School (Illinois, North Shore) track coaches in 2005. Rick Wolhutter and Peter Snell sat next to me, both Olympic stars and 800-meter run world record holders. In 2011 I was inducted into the Northwestern University Athletic Hall of Fame, quite an honor. In 1969 I was awarded the Big 10 Medal of Honor. Only one is given at each Big 10 school to one athlete out of ALL the varsity sports. What a long way I had come since Evergreen Park High school. How did all this happen, to an ethnic Polish-German kid from the South Side of Chicago growing up from 1947-65 in a Slavic neighborhood?

THE BEGINNING:

I was born in an area called Back of the Yards, at 55th Street (or Garfield Blvd.) and Ashland, about four miles west of the University of Chicago and about eight miles southwest of Downtown Chicago.

Chicago

A beautiful Lakefront. 3 million people and 9 million in the entire metropolitan area. Named the "City with Broad Shoulders" by the famous author Carl Sandberg. I had my start in track in high school when the track coach saw me running and said "You, I want you out for track". And so it began.

High school relay team. I am on the right.

US Steel

Growing up I remember the smell of gasoline fumes blowing in from the massive oil refineries in nearby Indiana. I liked it and to me it was a clean good smell, and a reminder of the industrial power around Chicago. I also liked to drive over the big bridge by Lake Calumet Port with my parents and look in wonder at the massive industrial plants on the Indiana-Illinois border and all the ships carrying grain from Midwest farms. I still do. It was exciting and indicative of a strong secure city and country without all the self-doubts of today. We also burned coal for heating in this large cast iron furnace in the basement. I helped my Grandpops shovel the coal pellets from the coal bin into the burning furnace and empty the large embers called clinkers with a big pair of tongs. I liked the odor, the deep black color, and the texture of the coal too. Things were really different then.

ME-Mom kept me well groomed

Age 13 Summer League Baseball

Played every summer, loved the game.

Father and me in 1984 Richard Schultz

American Prisoner of War Battle of the Bulge 1944-sent to a Stalag, German POW camp

Lutheran Cemetery Blue Island Illinois

German relatives arrived in USA from West Prussia Germany in 1885

My great grandmother migrated here from Poznan Poland in 1882, a kind classy woman

Museum of Science and Industry

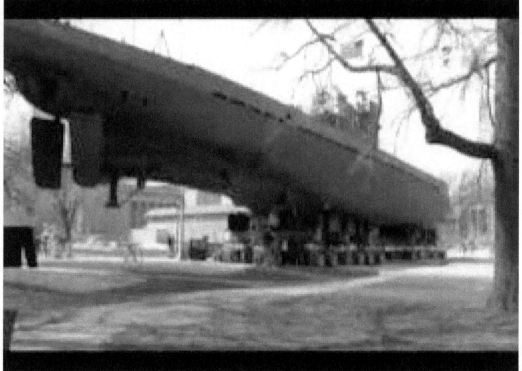

THE U 505

Captured in 1944

WWII German submarine at the Chicago Museum of Science and Industry-1954

As a 7 year old boy I was awestruck and amazed at this boat being pulled across Lake Shore Drive to the Museum. I have been in it recently at the Museum exhibit. Excellent visit.

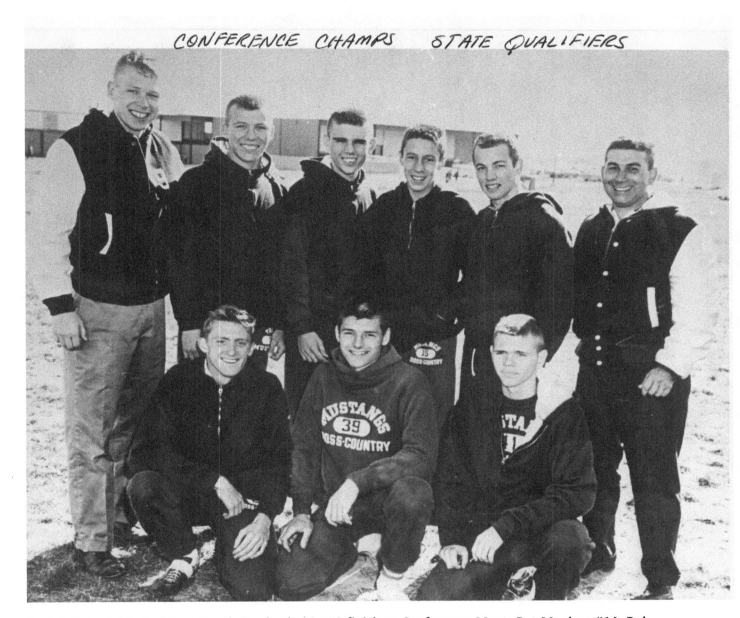

Back left to right: Assistant Coach Storbeck, Me #8 finish at Conference Meet, Pat Meehan #14, Bob Zander #5, Jim Limber #16, Coach George, Front: Alan Kloos #2, Ed Polaski #1, Bob Riley #4 Total points 20-a long standing Conference record --1963

PALOS FOREST PRESERVE RUNNING PATH-BEAUTY SERENE-MY FAVORITE PLACE

THE GREEN MONSTER GOLF COURSE HILLY FAIRWAY RUNNING IN SNOW DURING WINTER

THE UNITED STATES ECONOMIC SURGE OF 1945 to 1965

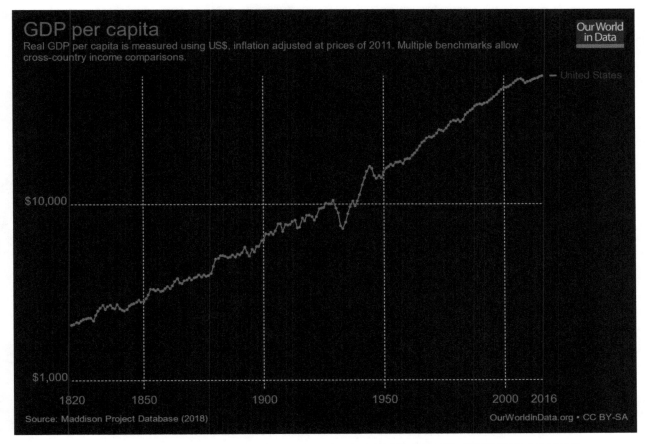

GDP per capita

Real GDP per capita is measured using US$, inflation adjusted at prices of 2011. Multiple benchmarks allow cross-country income comparisons.

Our World in Data

$10,000

$1,000

1820   1850   1900   1950   2000   2016

— United States

Source: Maddison Project Database (2018)

OurWorldInData.org • CC BY-SA

THE MIRACLE US GDP PER CAPITA GROWTH OVER 200 YEARS-STANDARD OF LIVING SOARS So now we are going to change directions and talk about the _SURGE,_ the economic and societal environment, after WW II. Then I'll finish with some of the highlights of my career from age 14-24 and a few other observations. Remember today I am an economics instructor at _Central New Mexico Community College_ and was a history major <u>at Northwestern University,</u> had an A average in history. A great school and history department. <u>Robert Wiebe</u> was an American history professor who really inspired me. Believe it or not I wrote a paper under his guidance called "The Economic Aspects of Social Change" And I still have that interest today. 50 years later. I'm always looking hard at world events, news, and am a truth seeker. I am also very interested in Russia. I put the concept of the SURGE in this book because it reflects the feeling of growing up in the 1950's and 1960's, which influenced athletic ideals and performance. We looked outward with optimism and ran for honor and glory-no lucrative stipends, endorsements, and training camps in those days. We were lucky we got a few pairs of shoes. I had to ask the Puma rep for a pair. And no performance drugs either. Great track and field athletes today can become very comfortable financially with some incomes over $100,000 to $1 million dollars plus. It's "Show Me the

Money! "But I can't think of one reason the shoe companies should make huge profits and not share it with more athletes. In fact, the second tier athletes, those ranked 4th-20th should ALSO GET FREE TRAINING, room, board, a moderate stipend and a part-time job. The Cult of the Celebrity Athlete, Movie Star, permeates American society now. Those at the top make enormous sums, while the rest of us struggle along or earn more reasonable incomes. Unfortunately, that's the currently popular idea.

We need to balance that out for America to achieve steady economic growth and opportunity for all as in the 1945-75 years. We need more inclusive training camps. Hello NIKE? NEW BALANCE? ADIDAS? And other major companies and wealthy people? And let's try a little more cooperation and less cutthroat competition in society. It would be better for everyone. Right now I am thinking about the University of Chicago Track Club run by the venerable Ted Haydon from 1960-1985. The Club, a real democracy, and a kind place, open minded, accepting.

IN EVERGREEN PARK TODAY

Anyway, today, August 2016, my friend Merrilyn and I are driving in Evergreen Park (our former home town where we graduated from high school) at 92nd and Troy, heading towards where the Aqua Park (community swimming complex) was or still is. I used to walk this street. I used to walk home from Aqua Park all summer as well. That was a two-mile walk each way, or I'd ride my bicycle. So I was always biking or walking all summer. Occasionally I had to run home when in high school, about a mile, to make my 10 PM curfew. Ran like the wind, sweating like a steam engine. Did this constantly - so it's interesting. That's part of this whole phenomena of moving, being full of exercise. And not always driving around in a car. Evergreen Park is a suburb adjacent to the Southwest corner of Chicago.

We stopped by the Evergreen Park High School track where I used to run and the area around the high school---The prairie and open space were behind my home where there were trails and we used to run and play explorer and do adventuresome things. Look, here's a park I used to play baseball in too. I used to walk a mile or two each way or ride my bike to middle school, 7-8th grade, age 13-14. And no rides from any parents in those days. Uh-uh, no way. I was more fortunate in High School –had about a long 2 block walk over some Grand Trunk Railroad tracks. The Grand Trunk is long gone. America's 15 or so railroads in 1960 are now combined into only four mega railroads. It's not as interesting as when each railroad represented a unique characteristic of its region and had their own logo and colors. When I was

12 we used to leave pennies on the rails and watch those freight trains roar by and flatten the coins. Speaking of trains, I have just gotten a 1970 Lionel model electric train, can't wait to put it up and just watch it run, round and round. That's what old guys do. Hah!

But anyway, there it is. The pool, the parks, the track, the schools, all these places where I grew up. It hasn't changed at all except the trees are bigger, forty, fifty years of growth. A few new houses, but not real new ones. They all look the same as in 1965. Yeah, I see it, I feel it. The pool, it hasn't changed. Three big pools, different sizes: big, medium and small for kids. Huge diving boards. Look at them. Slides. And it was all we did. There was nothing private. I mean, it was a public place for the community. I can still smell the chlorine. Yeah. Well, the pool has no water in it. And it has weeds growing all over. It's not being utilized. They used to sell inexpensive family memberships to it. But in any event, there it is. It's a ghost town. Part of the conditioning was getting a suntan over the summer and the long long trek to the pool.

So the town, the community of Evergreen Park, where I grew up, I see it as a continuing surge of labor, work, striving. It was and still seems to be a surge that represents industrial ingenuity and opportunity, success, stability. *IT'S THE MODERATE MIDDLE CLASS THAT AROSE AFTER WW II.* It's progressed from generation to generation. It's the momentum, the engine, the power of the country really. This type of community, many just like it, really built the United States. It's the secret weapon or the secret formula, I would say, of this country. All the similar communities, towns, cities in the USA. I not only see it, I feel it. It may not be exciting, but it's reliable. So maybe it's not as much as impressive as the powerful military and national security state that gives us international influence and respect, but the people at home, going about their lives, building, succeeding, having a sense of freedom to grow and develop- that's the REAL POWER in my opinion.

Buckingham Fountain Chicago

So all these stores and parks and people. And now it is my generation, us baby boomers, born in 1945-1963, that are running things. So here in Evergreen Park, Illinois, and similar towns are everyday people, some still here since 1946. Or their kids. And I don't mean that derogatorily either. Just responsibly then and now going about their business of life and learning and working. This is like a great stabilization power. It's the power that builds GDP, real economic growth of three or four or five percent a year, and not zero, one or two, speaking as an economist. No malaise then. And that sequence, that expectation that you would do better or well, and doors would be opened for making a good living and a good lifestyle, earning adequate money or more than enough ...trying a to lead a responsible life-- that was all available. It was. It's eroding now, at least that's what the experts tell us. And it becomes apparent in some places that the erosion is taking out some of the momentum and power very slowly. It's like a river losing its momentum over time, you hardly see it. But it slows down, gets less powerful. It drains off here and there. There's less water flowing into it from upstream. That's sort of what I envision this country as kind of going through. But the surge, that strength, you can still -- you can feel it here still. It exists in this area that we're driving through, Evergreen Park, Oaklawn, suburbs like it, Palos Hills, Chicago Heights. Yeah, it's more multi-cultural than it was, which is good because the country is too and things have changed. And let's not forget about cities like Milwaukee, Cleveland, Pittsburgh, Detroit, and Buffalo, full of hard-working immigrants and their children. I traveled to Detroit many times when it had a bustling downtown with tall buildings and and a buzz of business. It seemed to be like an Eastern city. I think the automobile companies gave it an international orientation and also a connection to Washington DC where executives went on important business. I liked it.

We see it here. The owners passed the house on. They transferred ownership. The new generations are here now. I see them here outside on the front porch or watering the lawn. the new and older generations, with still a possibility of a new economic surge. I think that it's the day-to-day momentum and the economic power that just builds, and it's kind of taken for granted that it moves people along the track of progress, whether it's socially together interacting or working together. It's this whole lifestyle. Today, too much of that gets diverted into much fewer upper income economic hands. Celebrity richness, opulence, people being told how great it is to be rich. But the dream then was, you see, not to dream about being there, or to become one of them. It's not the dream of moving from Evergreen Park say to a town like Winnetka, a very nice wealthy suburb (or Greenwich, Mclean, Shawnee Mission, Scottsdale, Gross Pointe, Shaker Heights). Though that may appeal to certain people.

But to most people then, the dream was just the good feeling of being within this surge of a positive life and not always looking out, wishing you had something else, but having what you want and developing yourself just a little bit more in your own life and with your relatives and children and so on, and grandchildren. So it's an organic process of being part of something you already have and not looking from the outside in, wishing you were elsewhere, SEARCHING for the American Dream, BECAUSE YOU ALREADY were in IT. The surge pulled and tossed us baby boomers out into the world full of hope and expectations that the USA would take care of us, give us a chance to show what we could do, live, give us a footing, a direction. Now I'm not so sure. It doesn't seem as clear.

READERS NOTES

What do you think about American society today?

What do you think about the USA economy? 2019

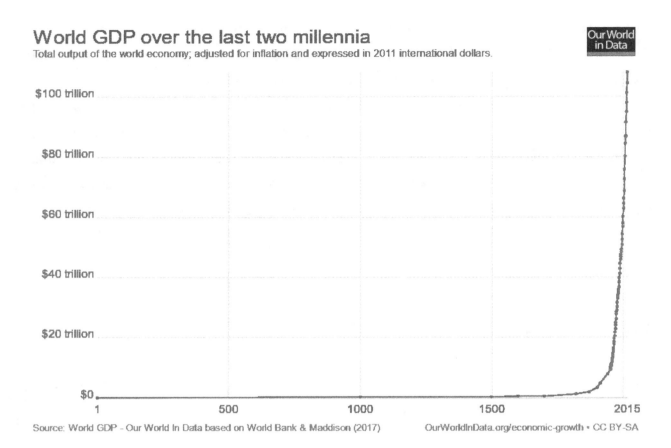

World GDP over the last two millennia

Total output of the world economy; adjusted for inflation and expressed in 2011 international dollars.

Our World in Data

Source: World GDP - Our World In Data based on World Bank & Maddison (2017)

OurWorldInData.org/economic-growth • CC BY-SA

Glory Days

Adjusted for inflation, average weekly earnings for production and nonsupervisory workers peaked in the early 1970s (1982-1984 dollars).

Recession

Source: Labor Department | WSJ.com

MEDIAN WAGE GROWTH USA 1970 -2015 DECLINE ADJUSTED FOR INFLATION FOR PRODUTION AND NON-SUPERVISORY WORKERS

Median Household income net of inflation unchanged since 1999.

Real median household income

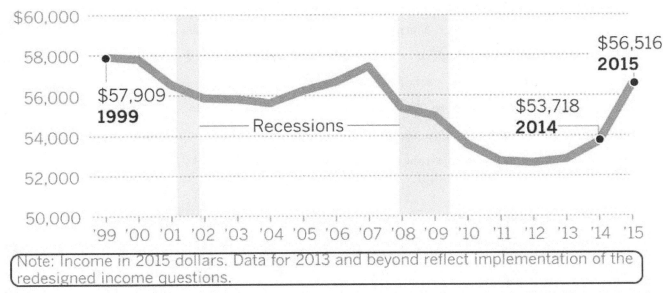

$60,000

58,000

56,000 $57,909
1999

54,000

52,000

50,000

—— Recessions ——

$56,516
2015

$53,718
2014

'99 '00 '01 '02 '03 '04 '05 '06 '07 '08 '09 '10 '11 '12 '13 '14 '15

Note: Income in 2015 dollars. Data for 2013 and beyond reflect implementation of the redesigned income questions.

Source: United States Census Bureau   @latimesgraphics

2019—estimated income per capita $60,000

I'm nervous about flying, and it comes and goes, the nervousness. As I get older, I don't fly as much, and I get more nervous. It's the insecurity of not knowing how it will go. I guess the flight, is kind of similar to living your life now and being increasingly aware of its insecurities and wondering how you will make it. But anyway, the whole world is going places today and tomorrow, across the ground at high altitudes and super-fast speeds. The USA doesn't seem so much a surge sometimes as a chaotic and random turbulence- gets you there all right, but the ride is no fun anymore for a lot of people.

BACK TO THE PAST----AGAIN

Summer 2017- another car drive through the Chicago South Suburbs

Okay. We're in Evergreen Park in the afternoon. I was just commenting on things as we drove around that afternoon in August 2017. Merrilyn Sweet, my friend is driving. Merrilyn took a left at the next street. Linda Dorl, another high school classmate came along too. She started a successful advertising business in Detroit, Michigan, part of the Surge. We're around 99th and Central Park. I was looking at the nicely groomed houses here. The impression I got is, you know, it doesn't look any different than it did 50, 60 years ago. But it feels safe. Everything is groomed, and it looks stable. It's just an intuitive feeling that came to my mind, strangely enough. Maybe not exciting.

So that's what I think, it just feels comfortable and safe. But it's the same homes. They're in impeccable condition. Exact same homes. It's like they just sprouted up out of the ground and were reborn. And the trees may be bigger, but it looks the same. There's some little trees. Some big trees. I don't really notice much difference going from a treeless to a large tree neighborhood over 50 years. There's some racially black people here, which we didn't have. Everybody in their nice tidy little homes. And there's a sense of stability here. That's what I said in my last outing. But I'm just saying it again. Compared to some of the other places, it feels safe here. These people are reliable. That's the feeling I have." How about you, Merrilyn? What do you think?

Merrilyn: "I'm surprised that it's the same, as you said. I'd like to go up to one of those houses, maybe one of the houses that I lived in and talk to them to see if they think the same way that I thought 50 years ago".

Ralph: "Yeah, here's the high school. It's, well, the enrollment is down about 30 percent, but it's a strong looking 1950s, '60s type of design. It looks solid, a strong edifice. And everything is neat and clean."

Merrilyn: "It looks smaller than it looked then, but the same type of appearance "

Evergreen Park High School-1400 students 1965

Yes. So we're moving now east on 99th Street. And I'm just talking away here, waiting for thoughts to come to me. There's the baseball field, and Merilyn's former house on Utica Ave. Here's the track and field and football field facility. A lot fancier than when I was a student, an artificial professional looking surface. Crossing into my old neighborhood now. Now here the trees look bigger. There's the house that's gone where your friend used to wait for you when you walked home. Slow down. Beverly Madrick's house. Tony the brick layer. Lenny the carpenter. Where's the old Schultz - Chubaty house? There's the Quinlan house. And here's the Schultz - Chubaty house. (Chubaty was my step-father's last name, it's Ukranian). We put a fence up there where I used to play in the vacant lot. Both baseball, whiffle ball, and bouncing a golf ball off the side of the house to practice fielding. On long warmer summer nights a bunch of us would play badminton. There's the house, 2911 W. 99th St. There it is. I grew up in the front there. Take a right. I'll show you where a friend lived.

UKRAINIAN ORTHODOX CHURCH BEAUTIFUL Icons Step-Grandfather attended in Chicago

Similar to my south side home, a typical Chicago bungalow, built in 1920's

All right. We're on Francisco, heading down along the road I used to run on those crispy winter nights. The house on the right corner is the old house. It's still there. That little, tiny house. Look at it. I'm surprised it's still there. The family was working class, very moderate income. The opposite of my classmates later at Northwestern University. The street had a rural small-town look to it in the past, vacant lots, small frame houses mostly. We played ice hockey there after school, pretended we were pros. Oh there's the Esposito place. They had a GTO Pontiac in 1966, a real hot fast car, full of chrome, a gigantic engine. Wow.

Well, we continued on down 99th Street, heading east into Chicago and into Beverly, which is a beautiful area. One of the more well-to-do parts of Chicago. It's full of woody areas and some hills and a Frank Lloyd Wright house. I used to run through there. It was exciting and connected to the forest preserve. I loved running through this different area of winding roads, unique streets, while sprinting and striding and running. I wonder what the people looking out the window thought. But to me, in high school, and then on vacations while in college, it gave me a sense of wonder and adventure and exploration. Similar to when I was a youth in the South Side of Chicago. That theme runs throughout my track career. Sort of a sense of awe in the environment I'm running in, the neighborhoods and what's happening in my life in terms of track and my future life out of college.

That evening we went on to meet Mike Rogalski, my high school friend, who I very much always liked. We had a great dinner eating steaks and pasta in a fancy Italian steakhouse and talked about old times. Merrillyn was there too. It's strange how decades go by but yet you feel as though you've known each other since yesterday. He is also part Russian. He needs to visit Moscow (WITH ME).

MIKE ROGALSKI AND ME IN CHICAGO 2018

READERS NOTES: What do you know about Chicago?

COMPETING IN TRACK IN 1965-1970

RACING for NORTHWESTERN UNIVERSITY AT UNIVERSITY OF ILLINOIS

Finish of Preliminary 1000 in 2.10 at Big Ten Meet 1969 night before world record. It felt easy

UNIVERSITY OF ILLINOIS INDOOR BIG 10 TRACK MEET 1969

FINISH 1000 YARD RUN WORLD RECORD 2:06   THIS IS IT!   THE BIG PAYOFF

RECEIVING THE 1ST PLACE MEDAL AT THE BIG 10 MEET

CTC'S United States AAU two mile relay champions. l. to r. Bob O'Co...
...en Sparks, Ralph Schultz, Lowell Paul.

jumped 16-6 to win the pole vault, John Craft jum...
51-7 3/4 to win the triple jump, Bill Cuello was secor...

1970--NATIONAL CHAMPION INDOOR 2 MILE RELAY TEAM----EACH OF US RAN AN 880.   BOB
O'CONNER, KEN SPARKS, ME, LOWELL PAUL.

We won again in 1971. Race was in Madison Square Garden on national television.

Donnerstag, 24. September 1970

Abendsportfest:

Die ersten Asse

sind schon da

Die ersten prominenten Teilnehmer für das Internationale Abendsportfest im Stadion (ab 18.30 Uhr) trafen bereits gestern in Wuppertal ein. Schon hier sind die dänische 800-m-Spezialistin,

US-Mittelstreckler Rolf Schulz, 800-m-Bestzeit: 1:46,6 Min.

Anneliese Damm-Olesen, US-Sprinter Charlie Smith und sein Landsmann Rolf Schulz (800 m).

Alle anderen Teilnehmer kamen bereits in der vergangenen

Zweita bei den Europameisterschaften: Anneliese Damm-Olesen

Nacht nach Wuppertal, oder treffen im Laufe des Tages ein.

Bis zum gestrigen Nachmittag hatte Organisator Paul Schurmann 100 Sportler-Zusagen.

US-Sprinter-Star Charlie Smith. Er lief die 200 m in 20,7 Sek.

Der 101. Teilnehmer rief am frühen Abend an: Volker Ohl, Deutscher Stabhochsprungmeister (5,20 m).

Zwei Amerikaner in Wuppertal

Erste Gäste des Abendsportfestes trafen ein

Der Hauch des „Sportlich-Internationalen" wehte bereits gestern durch Wuppertal. Das 14. Internationale Abendsportfest begrüßte seine ersten Gäste. Die Silbermedaillen-Gewinnerin bei den Europameisterschaften in Athen, die Dänin Anneliese Damm-Olesen, reiste aus Versehen einen Tag zu früh aus Kopenhagen an und nahm so den Begrüßungstrunk zusammen mit den beiden Amerikanern Chuck Smith und Rolf Schulz ein.

Über das bis zuletzt ungewisse Kommen der beiden amerikanischen Läufer freute sich Paul Schurmann, Organisator des Leichtathletik-Abendsportfestes, natürlich besonders. Der farbige Chuck Smith wird über die 100 und 200 Meter starten und nach Schurmanns Voraussage beide Rennen siegreich gestalten. Hervorragend ist die Zeit des Amerikaners mit dem deutschen Namen. Rolf Schulz läuft die 800 Meter in 1:46,6 Minuten und wird seinen Start in Wuppertal, trotz großer Konkurrenz, sicherlich ebenfalls siegreich beenden.

● Letzte Verpflichtung: Der Deutsche Stabhochsprungmeister Volker Ohl wird in Wuppertal ebenfalls dabei sein.

● Das Abendsportfest findet bei jeder Witterung statt.

Die Ersten, die in Wuppertal ankamen und die Favoriten ihrer Starts: Anneliese Damm-Olesen und die beiden Amerikaner Rolf Schulz und Chuck Smith.
Fotos: Peter Reis

German newspaper article in Wuppertal prior to International Track Meet August 1970

Eugene Oregon August 1970. Our American 2 Mile Relay team set an American Record at the University of Oregon track. I ran 1.48. 4 with no competition.

Los Angeles Coliseum June 1968 Olympic Trial Exhibition Track & Field Meet

RUSSIA

Red Square Kremlin in MOCKBA (Rus spelling). St. Basil Cathedral in background

The center of the Russian Government.

Red Army Star 1979

MY TRIP TO RUSSIA IN 1968 AND SOME HISTORICAL ISSUES

THIS SECTION WAS PUBLISHED IN MY PRIOR BOOK UP TO PAGE 57

I was officially invited to the Olympic try-out camp at South Lake Tahoe that summer to prepare for the Mexico Olympics. There were about, I think, 12 of us in the 880, maybe 14. I guess officially I was ranked about 6th overall in the USA. The idea was to acclimate to the 8,000 foot altitude in Mexico City and as well as to prepare generally for the Olympics, and for the try-outs, which were going to be held in the beginning of September. I had a dilemma. I had been accepted to go with the Northwestern University (my school) Russian Department for a study trip to the Soviet Union for 6 weeks in mid-summer (2 weeks in Leningrad, 3 weeks in Moscow, and then 8 days in Lithuania, Warsaw, Berlin, and London.). I decided to go on that trip. Why, folks? Because I didn't think my odds of being the top three to make the Olympic team were that good. I really wanted this trip to Russia because I was interested in Russia, international politics and issues. International Relations was a central field of interest of mine for a career. It was just a marvelous trip. We (a group of about 20 students and 3 professors) went there and flew a part of the way on the Russian airline, Aeroflot, into Leningrad one morning. And I still remember this. The plane landed, it might have been a smaller airport or off to the corner. And we got off. It was 6:00 in the morning, cool, a little hazy, foggy. And right there on the runway next to the plane there were five Russian bureaucrats or agents waiting for us, all dressed very drab, in the same style gray trench coats, not smiling. I think three men and two women. And basically, they looked us over and looked through our suitcases to make sure we didn't have any religious materials, and you're only allowed so much money, dollars that is. Their official welcome was very austere. And I guess that's the Soviet Union for you. We took a bus to a town about 20 miles outside of Leningrad where we stayed at a Workers' Resort. Now this was not a resort the way we in the West think of it. It was basically like a college campus. It was an area full of dorms, a big dining room area, a meeting area, a movie theater, volleyball courts and basketball courts outside where the workers came for a designated free vacation for a few weeks. Of course, everything was free and the activities were organized. This was a feature of the Soviet Union building an egalitarian Socialist-Marxist society. And it wasn't posh. It was like a small standard state university built in the 1950's here in the USA. We stayed in the dorms. I had my own room. We shared a bathroom. It reminded me of my freshmen dorm at Northwestern. It was our base of operations. We took a bus into town every day to study Russian. Our woman teacher pushed us and was strict, calling on me when I lost focus. And then in a lot of the afternoons, we went into Leningrad and roamed around. It was just a fantastic experience. I remember once going by a shuttered church, but there were all kinds of flowers put down outside so the people still worshipped. They just weren't allowed to practice it in public. An interesting thing was that there was a small building, like a hut, there on the resort campus. In it there was a bar. It was very simple. It was not exciting. There was a jukebox with some American tunes. And Tom Jones was on it. It was played over and over again. It was their favorite artist. The bar had simply a minimal amount of alcohol of different sorts, mostly vodka. I don't recall there being any ice. It was very plain. There were some tables scattered around. We spent time in there talking. We met some of the other foreigners, most were from Finland. And none of the Russian vacationers were allowed in there strangely enough. So it was just for foreigners, which I thought was kind of interesting. Candidly, Russia was a drab but stable society. No commercial advertising, neon signs, fast food restaurants, no traffic, and few cars, all small black ones. Clothing was not fashionable either. But I liked the country. And very little crime.

As far as training was concerned, I diligently trained, if not every day, close to it. And at this phase of the trip, the first two weeks, I did my running out around this Workers Resort, which was along the Gulf of Finland, this beautiful ancient looking beach with pebbles instead of sand, the sun still glowing some at the northern horizon at 1:00 am. I remember some nights, I would run up and down that beach into that setting sun at 10:00, 11:00, 12:00 at night. The sun glowed over the horizon almost all night. And I would just tear down that rocky beach, run as hard as I could. How far did I run? Oh, I don't know. I probably ran a mile in one direction fairly fast, pushing it, and caught my breath for a minute or two, and ran back. And down there were fishing homes, like cottages, right on the beach. These homes were made of wood with porches carved with designs and flowers. It was going back in time. The fishing boats were pulled up on the beach, made of wood, with a sail, and had the sailing masts sticking out of the middle of the boat. They were maybe 30 feet long and 8, 10 feet wide at the most. Just going back in time. But it was just a marvelous feeling. Not many Americans experience that. Far from the modern crowded life in the USA. You know my ethnic descent is from northern Europe along the Baltic Sea. I am a forest Baltic person deep inside. I actually feel comfortable in this environment with small pine and white birch trees and extensive marshes, and the slight chilly breeze of the sea. A little bit

austere and serious, like many of the ethnic people who live there, the Baltics, Germanic Prussian, Finnish, Russian.

.

I had another running route. We were along the coast and there were sand dunes and intermittent forests and some meadows. So I'd rundown a road and then cut off it into these sand dunes areas, where I would do hard striding over flat stretches and then sprinting up and down these sand hills. And lo and behold, the World War II relics were there for what I believe was the Finnish-Russian War of 1939 and the WW II siege of Leningrad by combined German- Finnish forces. This was about the perimeter front line. And at the top of these hills were pill boxes, which were these round, concrete fortifications with slits in them for guns to come out, and not just rifles, for artillery. And there was wire, old barbed wire spread around here and there that was used to stop the opposing forces from advancing. It was really a trip back in history and quite fascinating. I still am fascinated. It's a lot more than reading about it in history books. I relived it. Lucky me.

RUSSIAN PARTISANS WWII   NEVA RIVER LENINGRAD

The wide Neva River is beautiful in Leningrad, some of the Russian warships were parked there and submarines. It was just a beautiful setting. And I really was interested in, what we called, our enemy.

because to me I didn't have any enemies And now our US Congress is saying that again, hmmmm... I am disheartened that our Congress and the mass media are calling Russia our enemy. This is dangerous and not really true. The Russians want reproachment with the USA. The cyber hacking is a defense tactic, although that does not justify it. Portraying Russia as an enemy is a political construct by our government and what is now called the Deep State and the Neocon attitude. The US Deep State is not happy with a centralized managed autocratic Russian "democracy", a powerful Russia (President Putin's words). They want a western style democracy that is not a rival to US power and worldwide influence. Russia is very concerned about this attitude and considers it an existential threat to their country. Being an autocracy and monarchy for 800 years, the transition to a western democracy will take time to evolve. And Russia is the biggest country in the world with 11 time zones. Without centralization, it would be very difficult to control and manage their country. The Neocon Deep State follows an aggressive US foreign policy that will willingly use military power selectively and exert influence over governments that do not conform to US strategic interests. Today they are also called Hawks. This is composed of many of the experts you see on news shows, former CIA officers and directors, generals, intellectuals, news experts, politicians including many in office now, and US officials. They believe the USA is the only exceptional country protecting the world from the bad guys, the evil leaders. With the exception of the madness in North Korea, I don't see any real country enemies. The USA has sponsored many autocratic tyrannical leaders when it is to their advantage. The Shah of Iran, President Pinochet of Chile who replaced an elected President Allende, 1973-1990, a Marxist, who did many constructive things for Chile, and guess who, Sadam Hussein of Iraq, a real tyrant, but who attacked Iran in a 7-year war 1979-1987. But Iraq was mostly a secular state friendly to Europe and the USA, a stable outpost for USA policy and a real buffer against Iran who was reasserting itself as a mid-east power after the 1979 revolution that overthrew the Shah of Iran, another dictator, and an ally of the US. Learning all this history has caused me some disillusion, but I still think the US is a great country but has been gradually losing its way. Watch Oliver Stones' long documentary, *The Untold Story of the USA*. My ideas were not gained from this all-encompassing movie, but coincidental and formulated over a long time of reading, studying, and thinking. Oliver Stone, a great director, produced *Platoon,* an anti-war movie about Vietnam staring Charlie Sheen in 1978, my favorite movie. Very realistic war movie depicts its horror. And us baby boomers know here again the US backed a ruthless corrupt dictator in South Vietnam. North Vietnam was defending their freedom after being dominated by the French since WW II until 1954 and then a series of USA South Vietnam puppet governments. What a terrible waste for all of

Vietnam and the US soldiers (58,000 killed). North Vietnam lost 2-3 million civilians and soldiers. I have a high school friend, a basketball team athlete, who joined the Marines as a patriotic citizen and was killed there after 2 months. It is time for the American people to get educated about the reality of USA foreign policy. It hurts. It is the law of unintended consequences causing great harm. People it's time to assert yourselves! And Oliver Stone invite me out to California. Anyone care to join me? By the way you don't have to accept what I say, find the truth and your opinion your own way. By writing this section I know I will be alienating some people, maybe the US government. Hello FBI. But I am 70 and have early stage bladder cancer (it's ok now). I need to speak my mind. You younger people and leaders, God bless you, try to be rational and assess all the facts from all viewpoints before making a judgement, an opinion. I have great faith in the independently minded Millennium Generation, ages 18-35 in both the USA and Russia. And watch Oliver Stone's recent 4 hour interview of Vladimir Putin (on Showtime). President Putin appears very relaxed and candid with a sense of humor. Oliver has a kind questioning respectful demeanor, maybe a touch naive. Putin is very shrewd and well informed and disciplined.

The USA feared the spread of the doctrine, Communism, that said capitalistic countries would cease to exist due to economic evolution, peacefully. The violence of the Soviet Stalinist period in the 1930's created fear in the minds of Americans (and Ukrainians). But also remember Russia was also afraid of the West and America. Germany had just destroyed the country in two World Wars. WW II had ended 23 years ago in 1968 when I was there. The Cold War was on. The USA had many nuclear weapons on B52 attack bombers just outside the Russian borders, a 1-hour flight to Moscow and minutes to Leningrad. A little scary if you ask me. Remember the movie, Dr. Strangelove?

And the Aeroflot Russian passenger jets! Yes, the Russians were prepared militarily if invaded again. They were twin jet engines, what I would call "nimble and sporty". And the nosecone under the cockpit was transparent, a bomb site! These aircraft could be converted quickly to bombers if needed! Inside they were Spartan-plain canvas seats without foam padding, they looked like a military transport, and felt like it.

We took busses into the rural areas. There were these beautiful little homes made of wood. They were one story cottages, called Dachas, with flowers and gardens all around them, very quaint with the typical, old European woman, standing outside smiling. One time a part of our group took a bus on a Sunday about a 30-minute ride to the Finnish border and got out and wandered around this small town, taking pictures. And a man came up and said, "Come with us. I want to take you and show you the library and museum." And when they got to this building, lo and behold, the library was the local center for the Communist Party headquarters in that town. They were interviewed for several hours and their film was taken because right there was a ballistic missile base along the Finnish border, a defense fortification or offense, depending upon your point of view.

So I went to Moscow for three weeks. And my memory is a little vague. But I remember jogging to a nearby park, joining a man my age playing basketball. He was studying to be a diplomat. And of course, this is 1968, the height of the Vietnam War. He wanted to go to Vietnam to be a Russian diplomat in Hanoi. I thought that so fascinating. Here we are, I'm right up with somebody face to face, the opposing side, playing basketball with me. How ironic is that. But to me, there was no opposing side, as I have said. I sometimes wonder what happened to him. And I ran around this park. It was a combination of short, hard distance runs (2 miles or so) and fast smooth striding with short rest periods. But they were very intense. I wasn't just fooling around. I was training. We had a marvelous time in Moscow. One of the most interesting, fascinating places to visit is Red Square alongside the Kremlin. The Russian Government has the Victory Day Parade there every May 9th, the day Germany surrendered in WW II. This is a televised event on U Tube. Watch it. (GOOGLE Red Square 2018 Victory Day Parade English). You will see soldiers marching, weapons on parade, and President Putin making a 10-minute speech. The commentary is like CNN in English. Very clear. This event honors the Russian people lost during WW II and the defeat of German fascism. Russia lost 20 million civilians and 8 million soldiers. They gradually pushed Germany back from the edge of Moscow to Berlin from January 1942-April 1945. This broke the back of the German military. Alongside this beautiful square is St. Basil's Cathedral, the magnificent Russian Orthodox Church with the onion spires you have seen, multiple colored, and watching over the Kremlin. It was first built in 1331, a long long time ago. What I felt there in Red Square and still do when I see videos of it today, is a really a deep sense of the Russian soul, a deep sense of Russian history. Two Russian WWII songs you must listen to on UTUBE are *"Katusha"* and *"Farewell to Slavyanka"* This will give you a deeper sense of Russian traditional beautiful hopeful songs from the heart. You know Moscow began in 1250 and Kremlin means fortress. For 200 years the Mongol Empire conquered and controlled Russia, from 1250-1450. But they let Russia have a degree of self-governing. After 1450 the Russian Empire expanded and contracted, waxed and waned. You can seem to feel a sense of history. There is just this tremendous sense of power. I know the Russians have a very strong connection to Mother Earth and Mother Russia, which goes to their heart and soul, and is not nearly as obvious in the USA and Canada from what I can tell. It is an emotional historical connection. You can feel it there, *you can sense this civilization is to be respected and politically a force to be reckoned with and handled fairly with equity.*

To get a glimpse of Russia today on a casual warm afternoon in Gorki Park on Victory Day after the Parade GOOGLE: "Real Russia" Gorki Park episode 47. It is very humorous. There are 146 episodes of

Real Russia that show a glimpse into Russian life today. Very interesting and not political. I recently spoke long distance to the film maker Sergei Baklykov.

Russian lady distance runner in the forest. Russians like their forests 2015

Contemporary Russian woman 2017

While we are on this history lesson did you know Lithuania and Sweden occupied Russia and came up right to Moscow in 1610. In 1708 Sweden and Poland attacked Russia again and came within 10 miles of Moscow before being pushed back at the Battle of Poltava. It's significant that several Empires came so close to Moscow but had to retreat. (Napoleon/France, Germany, Sweden.). In 1650 Ukraine was split in half by Poland and Russian opposing forces. Conflict and outside control there is not new. Far western Ukraine was once part of Poland and also Austro-Hungary and sided with Germany when the Germany Army invaded Ukraine on its way to Russia. Borders change. The ancient Rus people originated in an area comprising parts of today's Russia, Ukraine, and Belarus (White Russia). Families today from all three countries are intermingled and the languages are almost identical as is their Russian Orthodox Christian religion. That area is centered on the ancient and current cities of Novgorod and Vladimir and has strong historical connections to Kiev. See, it's not so simple. And do you know that during a lengthy religious service lasting 2-3 hours all people stand. There are no pews, seats, benches! A Russian told me this to show respect to Christ and the saints.

Shut Orthodox Church with flowers in front

I hope to go back there soon to visit for a few weeks and meet some friends I've met on the Internet, Russian businessmen, some professors and economists, maybe a government official or two. I hope to teach a survey course in economics there and do some lectures on USA economic issues. I study Russian now. It's one of my sidelights, Russian politics, history and the language. Who knows maybe I can give the Russian middle-distance runners and coaches some good advice based on this book. That would be good for all of us. I almost ran in a track meet in Leningrad in 1968. A Russian and Finnish local city club were competing. The 800 went in 1:50, won by a Finn. I might have won. This would have caused a big political problem for the Russian coach.

Let me tell you that it was a marvelous trip. But the interesting part from the training standpoint, which I'm sure you're all interested in, is I still trained hard. That was six weeks, really, of very intensive training, no interval work, no spiked track shoes, all in flats, running with a sense of inspiration, and with a tremendous amount of really, basically intensive fartlek is what I would call it. Around parks, on beaches, sand hills, meadows and farms. And to tell you the truth, it kept me in great shape. I was concerned about my conditioning. It just goes to show you, that you don't need to be running hard intervals on a track for most of a season to develop racing condition.

Some other key points about the trip I need to mention. Many people inquired if the USA was so great how come your leaders were assassinated, Martin Luther King, Robert Kennedy, and President John Kennedy. I had no answer. The Russian people said the American people were great, but the problem was your government. They still do. Wandering around Moscow one day about eight of us came across a small storefront with a big map of Vietnam taped to the window. And wow, it was the National Liberation Front or Viet Cong Embassy (those South Vietnamese fighting against the South Vietnam government). We were invited in for tea and chocolates and seated at a long table. Their representative gave a gentle candid talk about their point of view and said he was sorry some of us might fight there and be killed. It shook me up, but I was amazed to be having this diplomatic experience while a war was raging half way around the world. We went to a ballet inside a theater in the Kremlin. In the audience were many Chinese high-ranking officials in those high neck stiff khaki uniforms with red epaulets. It was very strange to be in a roomful of people who also were considered enemies, anti-capitalist revolutionary states. And astounding to be with them right there in such a cultural peaceful place. Also the stores did not have cash registers, but used an abacus to calculate purchases, you know these round wooden balls on wires on a piece of wood. Several times young Russians asked to buy the blue jeans I was wearing for a high price and send them cassettes with The Beatles and other rock music. This was all illegal with stiff penalties. Ouch. The meat shop I went into had almost no meat. I remember a few large whole fish for sale. Consumer goods were shoddy. Shipments from Austria and Hungary had long waiting lines in the streets to purchase shoes. Appears free markets do work. President Putin said about 2012, "Russians who don't think back fondly about the Soviet Union have no heart. Those who want to return to it have no head." So true! Today Russia has a capitalistic free market economy somewhat controlled (managed) by a strong government. Hmmm...well maybe today the USA has a few somewhat similar characteristics. Corporations, big money, trying to do what is best for America, and themselves, exerting strong influence. What do you think? Consumer goods and everyday culture are the same as in Europe and the USA. We went into Lenin's tomb alongside the Kremlin wall. A very long line of

Russians waited outside. Naturally we didn't have to wait. Unbelievable, I actually stood along the real preserved body of Lenin under a glass casket, 2 feet away. As Americans casually do, I slouched and put a hand into my pocket. A soldier standing behind me uttered a loud command and pulled my arm out of my pocket and snapped it down! I was very disrespectful. Just goes to show you. Other things, absolutely no commercial advertising, but giant signs on buildings declaring loyalty to Marxist Russia, Lenin, and Soviet Workers and Soviet power. Also no world news except limited interpretations filtered by the Communist Party. When one of us brought back a Time magazine from the American Embassy we all read it cover to cover. There really was a news blackout. No visible restaurants and fast food franchises. Hardly any cars, but overstuffed busses, people squeezing in for a place to stand, all wore the same drab trench coats. At the hotels an older lady was in the lobby checking on you. You gave her your key, a big key hanging from a large wooden ball. Couldn't lose that. Statues of Lenin were everywhere. But the art in the old monasteries was dramatic, deeply meaningful on a flat surface and called an icon. We went to Zagorsk, an ancient monastery. Part of our group went on a quick weekend trip to Kiev, Ukraine. Get the connection everyone? Not a simple situation today.

LENIN'S TOMB Red Square--Founder of Soviet Communism

But do I remember the delicious Russian ice cream sold by women street vendors from their carts! Each piece was slightly different, seemingly hand made. You would love it! There were also soda machines on the streets. With a weak fruit tasting fizzy water. You put in a few kopecks and pressed a button and your favorite flavor flowed out---into a plastic glass that was put back after drinking and reused by everyone! But it did have a rinse nozzle with no soap.

The schools. Then and I believe now, the students were very serious and disciplined. When a teacher entered the room, the students stood up. Yes, for real! English was taught to everybody starting in Grade 1. The teachers made you work. I studied Russian in a classroom for a month. I remember. No nonsense. Today high school in Russia is more rigorous than in the USA. To graduate you must pass a difficult exam. Ordinarily this takes up to a year of extra study and several attempts. So most students graduate in 5 years. Some exams are oral 1 on 1 student to professor. Ahead of time the student might be given 3 questions to study and not know which will be used for the exam until it begins. For higher education students are put into the "ACADEMIC" so called college bound track (about 1/3) and others into the Vocational track (2/3). Today many Russians attended vocational school and have productive jobs, important to building a socialist Soviet society then and now a free market economy. Many people were granted their own modest apartments (by Western standards) after the demise of the Soviet Union in 1992 and still own them today. They were owned by the State during the Soviet era. They pay only for utilities. These 2-bedroom apartments are about 500-600 square feet and a 1 bedroom 300-400 square foot, ½ the size of US apartments. But they are comfortable, but look tired, a little run down. Outside they all are a boring similarity, as Soviet authorities tried to create an egalitarian socialist state in the past.

I have a Ukrainian-Russian student from Donbass, the conflict area. He is very disciplined intellectually, age 20, and in the US Air Force. Arrived here at age 13. He said senior math in his American High School was the same as he had in 7th grade in Ukraine. The US has dropped to #38 in math internationally. Russia is about 20th, behind the Scandinavian and Asian schools. The US is 24th in science for age 16. Do you think education is critical for the future standard of living? I recently went to a Russian picnic here and met two professors of mathematics and a physics professor. All middle aged and schooled in Russia and now teaching at University of New Mexico. I am impressed.

My Russian Language Teacher 1968 Right: Today old Moscow Soviet apartments

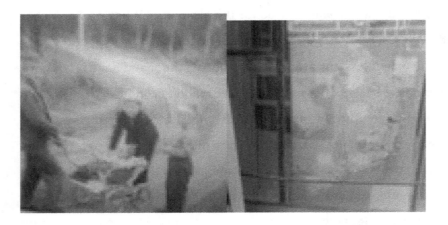

Boys near Finnish Gulf --Viet Cong or National Liberation Front Embassy map of Vietnam conflict 1968

Well, the trip to Russia began to end, and we flew to Vilnius, which is the capital and ancient city of Lithuania. A wonderful place. Here we met a stranger who attached himself to us, why I don't know. He had blond hair and German father. Probably a German WWII soldier. Whose surprised? He drove an expensive large motorcycle, very unusual in those days. Our group used to talk about politics at night and he would say, hush, quiet, they might be listening. Strangely, he sent me a letter to my home in the USA some time later with a picture. A few years later in 1970 I was undergoing a top secret security clearance for an army intelligence post. And guess what. The Defense Intelligence Agency knew about this and asked me a few questions! Still amazes me. Some might say I and some of the students were being sized up as possible Russian future sources. Russia has always had a very effective intelligence service. What if I or another student had a long career in the US Foreign Service State Department and maintained an open mind to Russian ideas?

Then we took a train, a Russian train. It was a steam locomotive with a giant red star in front for the Soviet Union, just like you saw in *Dr.Zhivago*, the movie. IMPRESSIVE!! And it was just marvelous going on this train across Europe. We stayed in a compartment for 6 people facing one another. Outside was a passageway alongside the train windows which were often open. No air conditioning. The interesting point is that when we got to the Polish border, which was in a bucolic beautiful meadow, there was a trestle overhead, and there were actually armed soldiers marching back and forth. And it really surprised me that these two countries, which were part of the Warsaw Pact, joined together, would have such an autocratic, highly threatening border patrol. We spent an hour there

while the train was investigated. We also had to show our passports.

Glory to the Soviet Teacher (translation) 1968

SOVIET WOMAN 1980

I couldn't understand why that would be. But it shows you something on the strictness and the tightly wound Soviet system. It wasn't all that friendly. But looking out, maybe a quarter mile out there was an old small church with a spire. And believe it or not, a woman dressed like, what I would call, folk dress, with a babushka over her head, was on a hay wagon being pulled by some horses on a dirt road in a meadow. I couldn't believe it in that day and age that is how agriculture was being done, a hay wagon pulled by horses. I also visited a Russian collective farm which was very modern, clean, and tidy with a large staff of workers trained by the Russian state to farm. They had new tractors and modern mechanized farm implements. But agricultural output could not keep up with the USA.

We stayed in Warsaw 2 days. It had more luxury goods and appeared better off than Russia. The Soviets had built a large spiraled pointed skyscraper office building in the city center, what the Poles called their gift from Russia. The Poles were not happy being controlled by the Soviet Union. But the Food!! What a difference and improvement from Russia. In Russia most of the meat was non-descript plain fried cutlets of some sort. We called it mystery meat. The vegetables were peas, carrots, cabbage, pickled beets often mixed into a salad with a sour cream like dressing and boiled potatoes. It tasted good but the meals were monotonous. And all were served with Black Rye bread. But the beet soup, Borscht, was delicious! But when we arrived in Warsaw, we were treated to a feast identical to the wedding banquets I had been to as a child in Chicago. Steaming plates of ham, beef, polish sausage, mashed potatoes, gravy, carrots, cabbage, and breads and rolls. Wow!

We moved on. We pulled into the East Berlin station where the train line ended. I remember I saw some Russian soldiers out the window, and I shouted how are you soldiers in Russian and one of the soldiers turned and looked at me and shouted back. Then we spent some time in East Berlin, which was totally bombed out. It still looked like it hadn't been rebuilt since World War II. Empty areas all over. No new buildings. Whereas West Berlin was a bustling beautiful commercial city full of people with handsome clothes. And there was a giant Coca Cola sign as we moved from East to West Berlin through the Vandenberg Gate. It was just totally amazing. I actually liked the buzz and the excitement of this giant neon sign after having none of this for 5 weeks in the Soviet Union. The other amazing thing there was our visit to the Olympic Stadium where the Olympics were held in 1936 during the Nazi/Hitler era of Germany. I just remember it as being an immense stadium. It had a sense of grandeur and power to it, which is representative of German culture. Just awesome. Here is where Jesse Owens of the USA, an African-American black man, won his gold medals. And remember he interviewed me when I was in high school. So ironic. I just wanted to run a lap around the track.

Well, we moved on and went to England. And the running part I remember there is that I stayed for a couple days on a farm. And what I did is I ran around the edges along the fence on a slightly lumpy pasture grassy ground. There were cows grazing in the middle. I ran fast 440s in flats, really pushed it. I guess it was about a 440, thereabouts. Real intensive fartlek or speedplay workouts a few times. The area was near Tunbridge Wells, a beautiful quaint area of narrow roads with stone walls alongside, and village inns. Nothing quite like this in the USA.

Echo Lake Olympic Training Camp Site at 7300 feet near South Lake Tahoe California. Note track built carefully in a forest to preserve trees. 1968

LAKE TAHOE

Well, the summer was coming to an end, and so I flew back to Chicago. I literally spent a day there and hopped on a plane, with my paid ticket from the Olympic Committee, to Reno, Nevada and then took I a bus up to the South Lake Tahoe training facility, which was about 20 miles up at Echo Lake at 7,000-foot altitude just south of South Lake Tahoe, a beautiful area. Since the Olympics were in Mexico City, at 7300-foot elevation, the Olympic Committee built this training facility. The airline lost my luggage which was a bad omen of things to come. We were housed in trailers. I had a roommate. But I tried to cram in too much running in two weeks to get ready for the try-outs. In the mornings, Mark Winzenreid and I jogged on a trail through some rocky area, through a forest near Echo Lake. And then I did interval work on the track in the afternoon. It's hard to remember it all exactly. But one thing stands out is that four days before the Olympic try-outs, my coach Bob Ehrhart showed up. And I guess I wanted to tune up with some 400s, but I was a little too pumped and I ran them both in 48 and a 49 with about a five-minute rest in between, which is really fast for me, about the fastest I had ever done. Four days later, I think I was still tight from that, and I ran a real lousy prelim about 1:51+ and finished way in the back. I just didn't have it. Then I went back home to Chicago. But then two days later, I came down with mononucleosis, a very serious strep sore throat. Maybe I was getting weakened, that I did too much all summer. And by the time the try-outs came in early September, I was really finished, getting stale.

It was quite a nice time though being with all those athletes, eating in the mess hall they had built up there. They had built a training camp and the track. There's really a beautiful forest. They have trees running alongside the track. Some of you will remember that very well. I remember that was where I saw, we went down to South Lake Tahoe, a bunch of us in some cars and saw the movie *The Graduate* in a drive-in. So every time I see that Dustin Hoffman movie, I remember this time very well. I was also becoming the uncertain graduate soon.

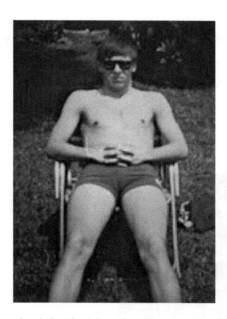

Fort Lauderdale Florida relaxing vacation March 1969

Roosevelt Park Albuquerque built 1933 by Federal Government

US War Room World Center

By this time, I had joined the US Army Reserves in the Fall of 1970. I went to meetings on Monday nights. And that took up some extra time and energy and planning.

I had a Top Secret Umbra security clearance and was a geo-political strategic analyst. My small unit wrote a major yearly report about some international issue. In August we went to the Pentagon to finish it with all the secret intelligence we were provided.

.

My favorite running place, Palos Forest Preserve outside of Chicago

RUSSIA-the BEAR

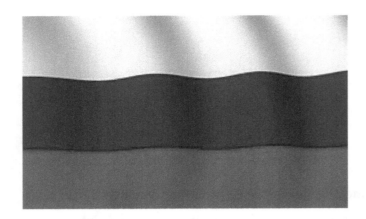

Kremlin at Night

RUSSIA is BIG

READERS NOTES:

How many miles across is Russia? Number of People? Miles north to south? Does this large size make it more difficult to govern?

Do you consider Russia to be an enemy of the United States? Explain your reasons.

If over age 60, were you afraid of Communism and Soviet Russia during the Cold War? Why?

WESTERN RUSSIAN EMPIRE 1914 Includes Poland, Ukraine,

KREMLIN RUSSIAN GOVERNMENT

RUSSIA-ISSUES TODAY:

The other point-of-view you don't see in the news. You decide.

Dispelling a few misconceptions that tend to mislead The American People

This section is NOT about the current leaders of Russia and the United States. (2019). It is about historical trends and geo-political issues that influence foreign policy today.

I speak about Russia again because I know something about it. It interests me. I was there in 1968 as a student at Northwestern University with the Russian department. We studied the Russian language and the culture and met all kinds of interesting people. I was there for five weeks in Leningrad and Moscow. I was an idealistic young man, somewhat intellectual, a history and political science major. So I really was interested in seeing another country, particularly one that was considered our enemy. Frankly folks, as I have already said, they weren't my enemy, and they still aren't. There may be government-to-government issues. But I don't believe in having enemies unless it's something clearly extremely threatening and immediate. I recently polled my economics class college students about foreign enemies. Out of 28 students, only 1 student considered Russia an enemy, 2 chose China, and 4 Iran. And there was some overlap. Another young 26-year-old said she didn't get what all this stuff was about the US having enemies. She didn't think so. So these Millennials are hope for the future. They don't have "existential enemies" like our US leaders and intellectuals, and the Neocons, the Deep State concept. The US and Russia just became afraid of each other due to certain ideological circumstances in the 1930s and 1940s and Stalin's purge of Russia and Ukraine. But Russians were and are a very kind people, and I enjoyed seeing how the Communists and Russian culture interacted with each other. I was in Red Square. It's a glorious, powerful place that goes back to past 1500. The Kremlin, which means fortress, is the center of the government. As I have said, and I'll repeat myself. I stood in front of Vladimir Lenin, the founder of the Bolshevik Russian Party in 1917, in his tomb, encased in a plastic bubble casket. You can see him. I stood two feet from him. I slouched, as Americans do with my hand in my pocket and a Russian soldier grunted something at me, yanked my arm out of my pocket and pulled it straight down and told me to be respectful. And that just said a lot to me. I remember another time I met a Russian young economics graduate student, who was probably two years older than me, about 23. We were talking about economics, capitalism, communism. And I was just curious. But what he said is, "We just believe our system, that means the Marxism/Communism state planning type of economy, in the long run will prove itself superior to yours. And yours will diminish." And exactly the opposite happened. But his commitment impressed me because it's interesting to see somebody who believes wholeheartedly and sincerely in something that's just the opposite of your own culture and economy. So we have to be aware of other people's attitudes. And their differences are just as valid, as long as they don't cause any direct harm to us.

I already spoke about some of my trip in 1968 and interesting aspects of Russia that I encountered. Now I am venturing into the more controversial, the current political and historical background of issues we see in the mainstream US news. Remember this is food for thought and not a hard and fast statement. I attempt to search for the truth as I encounter it, even if the result may be difficult to face. It is constructive then to find a mutually positive solution. A win-win solution.

Today, Russia is a complex country, and we need to join together with them to fight the terrorist threat and find some commonalities of interest, realizing we're different countries with different backgrounds. And we can't change Russia and make it like the United States. And they can't change the United States to make it like Russia. We just have to accept each other and realize we have interests that overlap and some that are a little contrary but not try to change the other but learn to live with them. I don't think American policy has done this. And sometimes ideology can really cause a lot of problems because you aren't always practical. You don't compromise. I tell my students that "entrenched ideology, or various "isms" kill, are harmful, cause strife, and big misunderstandings. So be flexible, countries are a blend of all systems. Be more of a realist and just do things that make sense for all sides, make a good deal. A win-win situation. And you can't get everything you want. Even Henry Kissinger believes that you shouldn't get lost in ideology, but just try to solve the issues of the time and to maintain peace and stability in the world. It's called Realpolitik. The persuasive educated well intentioned newscasters generally promote US policy closely and tend to omit important counter points of view. Look at professor Stephen F. Cohen, a Russian academic expert. He gets very little TV time to express a contrary minority point of view about Russian foreign policy, so the vast American public can make up their own minds. Noam Chomsky, a renown American intellectual linguistics professor from Massachusetts Institute of Technology, critiques American policies and gets zero press coverage. I think many reporters are so concerned about their careers they are afraid to deviate very much. Besides it's about ratings and network profits for their corporate owners. CNN is owned by Time Warner, a gigantic multi-billion dollar corporation which is trying to merge with AT&T, another giant. MSNBC is owned by the huge network NBC. These massive companies tend to inhibit risk taking contrary journalism, unlike the greats of the past like Walter Cronkite and Chet Huntley. It's the homogenization of the American news media. And corporate power extends into Congress as well. Congress virtually thinks alike regarding foreign policy, especially towards Russia. Except Senator Rand Paul, Kentucky, and two House Republicans, Thomas Massie, R-Ky, John Duncan Jr. R-Tenn. and two others. They opposed new Russian sanctions. That a way guys, stand firm. Vote: 530-5 for the new sanctions which are going to spell disaster internationally. Russia will retaliate. Solve this with diplomacy and reconciliation.

Regarding Russia it is not relevant whether or not they aggressively intervened in US elections with cyberspace tactics. If true, which US Intelligence insists, it was just part of being on the defensive against western encroachment, to get a less interventionist hawkish US president willing to at least consider Russian viewpoints. That doesn't mean such intrusion is acceptable. It didn't change the result of the election. President Trump ran a brilliant campaign. Russia is very concerned their way of life and independence is under attack. Is it? But interference in elections should never happen in any country. The Putin government is also restoring respect for Russia and some of its past glory and world status. So is China. The USA is already there and wants to continue being on top.

We also have to also remember what the Soviet Union accomplished. Russia built a huge industrial base from practically nothing, and an immense infrastructure of hydroelectric dams, power grids, railroads, highways, cities, schools, hospitals, and an exceptional space rocketry program (the first man and dog in space, Yuri Gagarin the cosmonaut, and Laika the dog).

Dog is pronounced "sue bach uh" in Russian.

So please remember, Russia has always been a country led by strong leaders and centralized power and control. For over 500 years the Tsar (KING in Russian) and the royal families ruled Russia with an iron fist for the most part. Dissent was barely tolerated. There is NO history of western liberal democracy that praises the status of the individual and challenges the leadership of the country. So why there should be now? The Russian people <u>accept a strong central state</u> which has protected them from outside invaders. The workers and peasants were uneducated, and a very small layer of wealthy people controlled the country (called Boyers in the pre-Soviet Tsarist era, and Oligarchs now). Income and power were extremely concentrated at the top. Like other European countries, China, Japan, and the USA, Russia was an Empire that expanded and contracted. It believed in its own culture and supremacy. It required respect. It fought numerous wars, like The Crimean War against England and Turkey in 1856 and lost. It fought Napoleon in 1812 and chased his army back to Paris. The Russian Army actually marched into Paris. Russia suffered tremendous losses in WWI, a war fought by the Tsar for the glory of Russia and the elite. When the Tsarist government was toppled in 1917, the Russian soldiers refused to fight and be exploited, put down their weapons, and walked back to Russia in the East, hundreds of miles despite officers attempts to stop them. The Bolsheviks were freeing the workers and peasants from oppression and a mindless war based upon European royal family rivalries.

WW II was worse. Germany flattened most of Russia and 20 million civilians and 10 million soldiers perished. Over 3 ½ long years Russia pushed the German Army back to Berlin (January 1942-April 1945). This began after the Russian bloody victory at the five (5) month Battle of Stalingrad siege (September 1941-January 1942). 300,000 German soldiers were captured in the frigid winter. The largest tank battle ever fought, with several thousand tanks, was in Kursk, Belarus in 1943. The defeat demoralized the

German Army and enraged Hitler, who had planned a major counter-attack to stop the Russian advance. German losses were heavy.

After a 3 year long (1919-1921) counter-revolution which was supported by Europe and the USA against the new Bolshevik government, the USSR was established. Unfortunately, the new Marxist Communist government became a rigid autocratic elite, in an attempt to perpetuate the socialist revolution. Marxism was originally a response to the terrible working conditions of the new factories built during the industrialization of Russia and Europe from 1840-1915. This set the conditions for the Russian Revolution. Marx was idealistic and believed in a worker's paradise in which the State would wither away. Well the opposite occurred. Russia became a tightly controlled State, ruled by the Communist Party elite (the new Royalty). People suffered (except for the elite) because they had so few consumer goods, and because the State economic planners ("5-year Gosplan" or State Plan) emphasized industrial development and military defense in an attempt to catch up to the West and build a prosperous and advanced socialist country. However, it is important to note the Communist state began with a very uneducated population of peasant farmers, and industrial workers trapped in extremely harsh working conditions with very low wages and benefits ("Proletariat"). The Soviet Union created an excellent educational system with a very high literacy rate (99.7% today). It built substantial housing units and provided free good health care for millions of working people. There were no homeless and everyone was given a job, no matter how minor. Crime rates were very low. I saw a woman drilling a concrete pavement street pothole. Women were also educated and became an important part of the professional workforce (accountants, engineers, doctors, teachers). I have a Facebook friend Anya, who is an architect, studied higher mathematics, was a member of the Young Pioneers (a Soviet Youth organization) and plays the violin. Her family were scientists, professors, and a high level Soviet Red Army officer. Another friend is a retired accountant and factory operations analyst. Svetlena, my Russian friend in Moscow, was educated as an engineer and worked on optics research for the Soviet Government (satellites?). Look at the advanced space-rocketry program technology, ahead of the West/USA at that time. As I said, the Soviet Union had the first cosmonaut, Yuri Gregaran, and the first life form launched and returned in a rocket into earth orbit, a dog Laika. The first satellite in orbit, Sputnik. And today the Russian Soyuz space launch rocket takes US astronauts to the orbiting International Space Station of which US astronauts utilize for research. USA space rocket transport rent is $490 million. This is a good example of the US underfunding NASA and scientific education.

In 1957 the USA was in a panic that it was behind Russia/USSR and began a massive science educational program. Unfortunately, Russia also had to create a massive military as part of the arms race with

European NATO and the United States. It is also too complex to plan an economy so tightly, because it suppresses the benefits of a free market responding to the laws of supply and demand. Shortages occur, and many goods and machinery are of poor quality as in the Soviet Union. In 1992 at the end of the Soviet Union, it was said that they had the largest industrial base in the world, but also the most outmoded and old, and inefficient. The free market system does it better, but it has its flaws. Today Russia is a capitalist nationalistic country.

There is also my Facebook friend Victor, who is for world peace and takes the Russian point-of view on foreign policy. He lives in Belarus. I have known him since 2014.

Now let's not forget, as I have said, and reemphasize, the USSR/Russia built a huge industrial base from almost nothing, and an immense infrastructure of dams, electrical power grids, railroads, highways, schools, hospitals, cities. But the Cold War took its toll as well and kept the Russian people in a perpetual state of fear of being destroyed by western Europe and the US/NATO. After all US nuclear armed B-52 bombers and nuclear armed Polaris submarines were minutes away from the Russian border constantly on duty, waiting to be ordered to drop nuclear weapons on Russian cities and military installations.

There still are I believe, some US military jets flying near the Russian border to remind Russia, that they can be attacked if necessary. Of course, now without nuclear weapons on board. That's why Russia does fly-bys of NATO aircraft and ships. You know a while ago a single US destroyer, the USS COOK, armed with sophisticated powerful missiles and communications equipment steamed towards the Russian naval port in Crimea and did not respond to Russian messages to explain their purpose and turn around. Russia flew some jets overhead very close by [reported in the US news as a Russian threat, no mention of US mission], and then Russia armed their cruise defense missiles and aimed, or locked on, to the US ship. The US naval ship turned right around and headed away out of the Black Sea. The US ship was another warning to Russia to back off Ukraine and intimidate the Kremlin. Also to boost the moral and will of Ukraine to fight Russia.

 The US had used nuclear weapons already in Japan in 1945, the only nation to do so. That fact has not gone unnoticed in Russia. It was not until the 1970's that the USSR had a nuclear capability that could match the USA. In 1986 Russia had 40,000 *large* nuclear warheads compared to the USA with 24,000. In 1965 the US had 30,000 compared to Russia with only 5,000 warheads. Now each country has about 5,000 which are at least 100 times more powerful than Hiroshima. One blast and a city the size of

Orlando, Florida, or Smolensk, Russia would be entirely incinerated. Total annihilation. Kaboom!! About 750 are actually deployed and immediately ready to be used by the US and I assume Russia is similar. The other 4500 are stored underground and disarmed, but they can leak radiation and toxic chemicals into the ground as they age which is a big problem. Also, as part of its defense Russia developed a superb intelligence service, the "KGB". It was like the entire USA FBI, CIA, NSA, DIA, (Federal Bureau of Investigation, Central Intelligence Agency, National Security Administration, and Defense Intelligence Agency) all rolled into one. The US combined intelligence budget is $80 billion plus $40 billion for Homeland Security. Now the KGB has been divided into two divisions, the SVR (foreign) and the FSB (domestic) but is being combined back into one organization. It is interesting to note that the KGB was a very elite agency that selected only top students and motivated loyal people as members. Then and now they considered themselves protectors of Mother Russia and the countries well-being. They are/were the "watchers" who made sure the country stayed on course. It was an honor to be a member. Through upheavals and changes since 1992 it has stayed the course and had a continuous autonomous existence, almost like a shadow government. Many of its high-ranking members are also involved in dual roles as executives in private industry. There is a flow back and forth. Some are closely connected to the central government. Generally they are called Siloviki which means force group. They are or have been members of the military (including military intelligence, the GRU) and the other intelligence agencies. They are intertwined with the Russian government and some key large corporate business. The USA has some similarities, but my hunch is that Russian security is more closely tied to nationalism and protecting the state. <u>Never underestimate Russia.</u>

After Communism ended in 1992 Russia became a wide-open disorganized state in which all State Property was auctioned off at very low prices and were purchased by investors (who became fabulously rich and powerful as the assets rose in price and were modernized). They are called Oligarchs. There were no democratic traditions, guidelines, and civil courts and laws to regulate business. High inflation wiped out people's savings and pensions and very high unemployment put the population in a very distressed situation. Many salaries were not paid for months including the military and civil service. The military was in disarray with equipment outdated and needing much maintenance. All of this was called "Shock Therapy" to quickly transition Russia from a structured socialist state to a westernized capitalistic economy and political system. American financial institutions and consultants like Goldman Sachs helped implement this policy and reaped huge financial benefits. Privatization of State business assets enhanced the immense concentration of wealth into the hands of Russian Oligarchs and neglected the welfare of most of the Russian people. This created resentment against the US. The Russian economy collapsed in 1998-99 and income and wealth decreased substantially. The Russian people could not understand why America did not help them to survive this horrible period. All this changed after President Putin was elected in 2000. The economy has been rebuilt with a healthy consumer sector based upon free market principles. The Russian Government bureaucracy has been substantially increased, perhaps by 100% since 1999. This seems like a throwback to the Soviet Union times. It also creates a loyal following of newly hired workers grateful to President Putin. There is some interconnection between large corporations and government policies. Oligarchs have had their independent power reduced. Russia is now exerting its influence around the world and on its borders as in the past. It has created a multi-polar world on a level with China and the USA. It is thought Russia has increased its agents in the USA since the Soviet Era, from 1000 to 2000. The number of Russian Federation domestic government employees has also increased very substantially.

A recent book and article by a Russian political scientist and advisor to President Putin, Dr. Sergey Karaganov, suggested the US has been in disarray and losing its power since 1994. That is when the huge divide began in earnest in US politics, Liberals vs. Conservatives. He has been an advisor to President Putin and now is Dean of the elite Moscow Higher School of Economics and Chairman of the Council on Foreign and Defense Policy. I saw him on CNN television being interviewed by Fareed Zakaria and have read one of his scholarly articles. Dr. Kargonov explains Russia is strategically concerned about military deterrence being adequate to deter outside aggression. That is also why Russia wants friendly buffer countries like Belarus, Ukraine, Georgia, and Finland along their border. Keep in mind the US has many, perhaps 25 or more military bases of size surrounding Russia and China. Russia has four naval bases, only two are outside its borders, in Syria and Vietnam, and not massive. The expansion of NATO to 28 countries since 1992 is a tremendous source of concern. So why is there NATO except to deter or intimidate Russia goes Russian thinking. You know in 1989 when Russian President Gorbachev opened up East Germany the US President George H Bush promised not to expand NATO eastward. That didn't last long. Presidents Clinton, Bush and Obama added many countries to NATO. That is a major "existential" threat to Russia which US newscasters and experts refuse to acknowledge. Also in 2002 President George Bush unilaterally terminated the Anti-Ballistic Missile Defense Treaty (ABM), which had been signed by Henry Kissinger and President Nixon in the 1970's. The US then put advanced anti-ballistic missile systems into Poland and Rumania and more are forthcoming. This upsets the balance of power. This was under the guise of defending Europe from an Iranian missile attack. That will take many years to develop that effective Iranian technology, if ever. If developed Israel will take it out. It sure looks like a defense against Russian missiles which will give NATO a tremendous advantage and make Russia militarily vulnerable. This perpetuates an arms race which is dangerous. Russia offered to work together to build a mutual anti-ballistic missile system in its southern border near Iran but the US refused to consider it. But we must remember the eastern Europeans fear Russia after seeing the brutal Stalinist period in the 1930's and the tight control of them by Russia as members of the Warsaw Pact, the strict economic plans that reduced their economic freedom, and the fear of secret police keeping track of people critical of the Soviet Communist State. Russia has a powerful military and cyber capability, so it is viewed as a threat. These new NATO nations take comfort being aligned with the powerful western European nations and the USA.

This provides national security, just in case something goes wrong in foreign policy. You never know.

Sergey Karaganov

In 2017 Russia began testing a new cruise missile and deployed 36 which might technically violate the INF Treaty of 1987 (Intermediate Range Nuclear Forces Treaty) that stopped the usage of Intermediate Range nuclear missiles which can reach all of Europe. (5000 km/3000 miles). It exempted missiles with a range under 500 km and all sea-based cruise missiles which the US has used extensively in the mid-east since 1990. Iraq twice, Syria recently (59 into an airbase, 1030 into alleged gas research centers), Libya, Kosovo and Bosnia. You can see how the arms race escalates. Russia feels it must catch up to the West's more advanced sea and air-based cruise missiles by having their own advanced model to be used over land in Europe to maintain a balance of power. Russia also has a highly developed defense shield over Europe and also a 3000 km advanced radar warning system out to the United Kingdom. It is defended by a ring of Iskandar short range offensive missiles with a maximum range of 500 km, (ok by Treaty) and anti-aircraft missiles extending outward from Russia 400 km., reaching from Turkey to Ukraine, to Poland, the Baltics, and the southern tips of Sweden (Stockholm) and Finland (Helsinki). (The economist p. 5, January 28, 2018). These are the deadly highly respected SU-300 and SU-400 BUK missile systems. Those countries might consider restraint in having a very aggressive anti-Russian foreign policy. Interestingly, Rumania, Hungary, and Bulgaria are not in that offensive/defensive ring. Syria is also protected by a ring of Russian SU-200 defensive missiles that can be replaced by the more accurate and deadlier SU-300. Iran has many short range missiles and the SU 400 defensive system. This entire area is called Russia's anti-access denial area. The Russians have been busy. Russian leaders want to restore the prestige their country lost after 1992. Vladimir Putin said, "the collapse of the Soviet Union is the greatest geo-political tragedy of the 20th century." Probably true unless you were a member of the Russian aristocracy in 1917. Russia in the 1990's was rejected by the USA as an equal partner and then faced an imposed international world order that does not serve nor acknowledge Russia's legitimate interests and nationalistic traditions, glory, international respect, and sphere of influence (Ukraine). Russia (and China) have invested substantially to rebuild their armed forces and develop soft power (cyber intrusive conflict). Russia's official national security statement considers NATO as their greatest threat and that the WEST is actively trying to create "color revolutions" in former Soviet areas (Ukraine, Georgia, Kyrgyzstan, maybe Belarus) and ultimately Russia itself to install a western liberal democracy and dissolve Putin's government. This is a large overriding Russian concern, hence the defensive and aggressive nature of their policies. By the way China is doing the same anti-access missile defense on its coast and has bombers, the H-K, that can reach Guam. And missiles and submarines that are configured to sink naval ships (the US Pacific Fleet). Hello USA. All of this sets the stage for a random event to trigger both a military and harsh cyberattack. Knock out satellites and invade computers to destroy a country's power grid and military command and control system and render it's military helpless. Remains to be seen. Can peace prevail?

The US is also developing dial-a-yield nuclear weapons that will generate a much smaller controlled nuclear explosion with a very accurate smart guided delivery system making their use more likely and encouraging a nuclear attack or threat to intimidate and control Russia (or Iran, or China) and disassemble their country into weak sections controlled by western powers. It also lends credence to the Russian belief that the West might unleash a preemptive nuclear attack. You say nonsense? Don't kid yourself-be realistic. There is a line of thought like this in certain people in the US Deep State and Neocon thinkers. Russia fears the Neocon anti-Russian attitude and world strategy and believes they are dangerous. The B61-12 dial-a-yield nuclear bomb can be adjusted from 3% to 12% the size of Hiroshima, or up to 4 times its size and power. The B83, the typical 1.2 megaton nuclear gravity drop bomb deployed ready to attack, is 100 times the size of the Hiroshima bomb. The B61-12 also has much better GPS targeting and can be launched from cruise missiles 500 miles away and hit in-ground missile silos, precise military positions, bases, key communications centers and infrastructure. Field commanders might also use them if needed to stop an advancing force. This makes them more useable as widespread damage can be avoided with less radiation. There is a US line of reasoning that a nation could launch a pre-emptive limited first strike and substantially destroy the enemy's ability to respond. The attacker would then be able to withstand the damage from a limited nuclear counterattack and then force the other side to surrender by threatening nuclear annihilation with its largely intact nuclear forces. I don't understand how this would work with undetectable nuclear submarines roaming the world ready to launch hugely destructive missiles. But anyway, it's scary to think about. After 70 years of nuclear parity with little real threat of nuclear weapons being used, now we are at a time when it might be considered as a doable and winnable strategy. There is not détente as in 1972-1989, which eased tensions between these countries and encouraged understanding and positive relations. And remember, if smaller dial down nuclear missiles are launched it may spontaneously lead to larger weapons being used. Russia has stated it will use small scale tactical battlefield artillery nuclear weapons if its homeland is threatened. But that is much different than the threat and destruction of a pre-emptive offensive strike. This is in their official strategic military plans. You can see it on the internet. The very fact some people are even reviewing this option is scary. When I look at these facts, it seems as if the West is misguidingly and perhaps purposefully threatening Russia and risking a major war. I won't let my son fight in it. Neither should you, my Americans. Stand up and be heard. Challenge the status quo.

Russia is also building a balanced multi-polar world. Since 1992, the end of the Soviet Union, the USA had been the unipolar power, until the past few years, when Russia reasserted itself (and also China). This is a problem or concern for many western leaders and intellectuals. As I have stated, in the US many are called the Neocons. They, or really this idea floating around like a VAPOR effecting many inside and outside the government, represents a more aggressive and militaristic US foreign policy that believes in extending US influence in countries all over the world. Some think the USA wants to "manage" the world for the world's own good in the USA's own image. They are the ones in the news always saying Russia is a grave existential threat and enemy. I don't believe it. And it seems as if the news media just goes along with this line of thinking. They primarily create news which doesn't present serious oppositional points of view. Remember Walter Cronkite, the iconic newscaster of the 1960-1975 era? He went to Vietnam in 1968 so see the war for himself and then back in the USA on national network news stated Vietnam is a lost cause, a draw, unwinnable. No one was saying that in the media. A month later President Johnson announced he was not rerunning for President. To make such a bold statement today is unthinkable. So Russia is not going to attack the USA or Europe or NATO with military force. But maybe with cyber misinformation. NATO has the same cyber capability. Russia is protecting its area of influence around their borders, and sometimes this looks harsh to the West. This is more like a rivalry and competition for prestige and world influence and respect. I had a lady friend in Russia who in 2015 said our two countries were vying for influence and just bumping each other around, like giant countries do when their interests conflict. Someone else said the Russian Government is unstable, which is a little bit scary. That is probably one reason why President Putin has so tightly controlled the Russian State. They fear chaos and are concerned about radical change. Remember many powerful people in and out of the US government believe in Regime Change. It is part of the Deep State objectives. So it is necessary to maintain the stability of Russia against outside western influence trying to uproot the government and create a western style democracy. President Putin forced all the numerous NGO's (non-governmental organizations) that were trying to do this type of thing, to register as foreign agents, with many connected to NATO countries. This has reduced their influence. The National Endowment for Democracy was kicked out of Russia which allegedly promoted western liberalism, democracy, and chaos within Russia funded by the US. USAID was also removed. These types of organizations promoted the "color revolutions" in Ukraine and other countries to install democratic regimes friendly to the USA and West. The USA put $5 billion into Ukraine over 20 years to create a western style democracy friendly to the West and not Russia. Ukraine and Russia have been connected culturally since the year 850. The Russian government fears it may be undermined and toppled by outside hostile influence. You think?? Would you like numerous Russian non-governmental groups to be operating in the USA, constantly criticizing and trying to diminish US type democracy and create a Russian type of centralized government. I don't think so. Let's be honest about this. The Russian Cyber interruptions into elections (alleged-but could be possible) are an embarrassment to US leaders and now they are mad as a hornet's nest splashed with a big bucket of water. In the Fall of 2016 during and after the US election Russia created over 3,000 Facebook ads (according to Facebook) that reached 11.4 million people, resulting in 80,000 posts that reached another 129 million people! The news networks say this is a threat to US democracy. To me the threat to democracy is policies like Congressional gerrymandering by the Republican Party that insulates their candidates from political challenges, and the US Supreme Court Citizens United decision that has allowed enormous amounts of money to influence US elections from Super Pacs, wealthy people, and politically biased intellectual think tanks. Just look at the distorted crude TV election ads, and the attempts to make voting more difficult for minorities and the poor with false narratives about voting fraud and the need for difficult to obtain ID cards and shortened election voting time causing enormous waiting lines. And the meta data collection of personal information. And the concentration of wealth in the top 1%-10%. And the increasing corporate economic monopoly power. And the attitude that anything military is always patriotic, honorable and should not be questioned. I respect the military, but it can be and should be critiqued. Remember I was in the Army six years as a strategic intelligence analyst. So then, what about social workers and teachers working in poverty areas as patriots? The Peace Corps? And research scientists working to stop dangerous diseases? Disaster area volunteers and forest fire fighters in California? These internal economic and political policies are a REAL enemy to democracy and a just society.

I want to also emphasize that the Deep State is not a conspiracy. It is a way of interpreting foreign policy outcomes. Many US leaders and intellectuals share the ideas of US supremacy to various extents and are good well-intentioned people. Their opinions on some issues can be substantially correct, but for the most part their general viewpoints are similar and highly influence a less than fully independent thinking free press.

Yes, Russia is probably disrupting some Western countries as part of their strategy of deterrence. It is not a good thing, but understandable is it not? The giant-sized cyber intrusion into the US in 2016 (according to US intelligence) is the greatest victory by Russia since the Battle of Bardolino in 1812 that stopped Napoleon's army. Or the Treaty of Andrusovo in 1667 when after a 13-year war, the Polish-Lithuanian Commonwealth ceded to Russia the fortress of Smolensk and Ukraine on the left bank of the Dnieper River (included Kiev). The Commonwealth retained western Ukraine. This part of Ukraine (eastern ½) came to be known as "Little Russia" and part of the "Near Abroad" by Russians, until this day (this is not considering the horrible somber destruction pushing back Germany in WWII over 4 years-30 million Russians killed-nothing to celebrate). So let the US set up strong computer firewalls to protect computer digital data, which the US must already have, and create their own type of Cyber influence in Russia if deemed important. I don't think the USA is about to fall apart. It is a strong country. And the Pentagon and CIA have not been hacked. Let's both take one step forward and discuss how to resolve our differences. Toss entrenched ideology out and find practical win-win solutions. And accept that Russia has concerns in their part of the world and is now an influential world power. Russia is also very worried about aggression from ISIS and Islamic militants that are relatively close to their southern border. Numerous attacks have occurred in Moscow. And the USA is listening, or storing in huge databanks, many of our conversations and tracking huge amounts of digital communications data. That is you and me, not just imminent threats. This book will probably go into a special US security agency file under my name in a gigantic server.

And also, let's not forget that Russia allowed the US to fly over its country and install an

US Air Force Base near Afghanistan allowing US airpower easy access to the war zones. Otherwise the flight distance from the Indian Ocean in the south would have been excessively dangerous and inefficient.

#MACD@Ralph Schultz -- *MUTUALLY ASSURED CYBER DESTRUCTION* --

Remember "MAD" IN THE NUCLEAR STANDOFF WITH THE Soviet Union? No one would launch nuclear missiles because it would cause a worldwide atomic catastrophe and destroy each other's country. What's this Tweet doing here? Just this. Today, August 2, 2017, it stuck me while watching the movie Snowden again. Remember he was the cyber genius working for the US National Security Agency collecting secret data who turned it over to Wikileaks and eventually fled and is living in Moscow the past 3 years under political asylum from Russia.

Folks we are at war with Russia, and China, and any other country or person who tries to hack into, interrupt, or shut down our communications and data networks. It doesn't matter which country starts it first. I believe that at this moment Russia and the United States are feverishly trying to hack into each other's data bases to gather secret information and install viruses to disable programs and applications. And at the same time trying to create cyber protective firewalls to prevent outside intrusions and maintain the integrity of their data. This is a 24/7 all out endless race. It's been said that Russia hacked into Estonia's major data and interrupted transmissions, the USA did the same to Iran, and someone recently attacked Ukraine. North Korea disrupted Sony Corp's US operations. I read the USA recently tried to install a sleeper virus into Russian government files. Could be. It will be. The technology to hack into US personal files by Russia to influence US elections is kid's stuff next to what could be done now or soon. A country, or even just a few rogue hackers, could upset an entire nation's electrical grid, knock out all electronic financial data, end the internet, cell phones, stop the operation of trains, planes, industrial factories, hospitals, distort data transmission of the US Defense Department. This has to be developing. Ever been outside during a power shortage crash during a rainstorm or heat wave. Everything at night is totally black and nothing moves. Now this technology must be kept at a parity or else if some country really gets attacked and loses, it is left helpless. Now that is war without directly destroying any property nor people. This is really scary. And to think you might lose all your saved pictures. Would the CLOUD help? Forget this talk of a cold war with Russia or any enemies anyplace. Someone tell me this is extremely unlikely. The only solution it seems is not to make enemies, to be real nice and make lots of friends. Perhaps a little naïve?

The new Russian hybrid warfare strategy deemphasizes extensive military conflict. The idea is to destabilize and discredit regions and countries with soft power like cyberspace and social media intrusion and influence, encouraging regional political unrest, perhaps a very limited military incursion (Georgia, Ukraine) if absolutely necessary to protect its borders. This creates some chaos and divisions and allows political groups to gain power that have favorable attitudes towards Russia. It also includes creating a strong diversified economy in Russia. This type of conflict is not costly, is flexible, and offsets foreign powers viewed as threatening. It neutralizes the gigantic US military advantage, with a budget of $700 billion versus Russia at $68 billion. Over a 10:1 difference in spending! The Russians are innovative and strategic.

And as far as how the government and President Putin have managed Russia, dealt with internal political competitors, the media, their elections, it is not the business of the USA, the United Kingdom, or Germany to try and fix it their way. Deal on a nation to nation basis on foreign policy. If Russia did not feel so isolated and fear the West's attitudes about it, much of the alleged Russian influence in Cyber interventions would begin to abate. This US/NATO national security fear by Russia might be present even with a new government as long as Russia is viewed as a military threat (which they aren't). How can a country that hosted the Miss Universe contest be considered a threat? You tell me. Russia likes President Trump because he wants to find peaceful solutions to issues and open up commercial trade with Western Europe and the USA. (this has nothing to do with the current scandal). I know a Russian lawyer and investment banker, Ilya, who is working diligently to encourage German business investment in Russia. He has Donald Trump's book <u>The Art of the Deal</u> on his desk. I saw it in a Skype video transmission to Moscow. IKEA, the Swedish household goods company opened 5 large stores in Moscow. Exxon has negotiated a $500 billion-dollar deal with the Russian national oil company Rosneft. I recommend allowing this joint venture as a sanctions exception. It would economically cement Russia and the USA and make any future diplomatic and military confrontations less likely. Russia is the largest oil producer in the world just ahead of Saudi Arabia and both have a large surplus of oil, unlike the US, Europe, China, and Japan, all of which must import oil to meet their large domestic demand. USA please let us try and figure out ways to initiate more peace and less militarism. We, the USA, have the world's biggest military at a yearly budget of $720 billion dollars, China $215 billion, Saudi Arabia $87 billion, Russia $68 billion. The USA military budget is larger than the rest of the entire world combined and the most modern and highly equipped, with outstanding soldiers. This is not enough? My political leaders in Washington, are you really afraid? Let's be realistic, with a balanced policy.

And remember, Russia is the world's largest country in geographic size with 11 time zones (the mainland US has 4 zones). That makes it hard to manage without strong centralized controls. It is the world's 6th largest economy, about a $4 trillion GDP (PPP basis) compared to the US at number 2, about $20 trillion. China is about $23 trillion at number 1. Russia is 48 times the geographic size of Germany. The Russian economy has some issues but it does not have the national high debt problem as the US and Europe, giving it financial staying power to sustain economic stress due to the 50% decline in the price of oil and political sanctions imposed by the West due to the Ukrainian issue. Russia is developing new internal industries and creating trade relations with Asia and China. Russia has a total debt to their Gross Domestic Product ratio of only 15%. The USA is 100% and much of Europe is 60%-80%. GDP measures the size of an economy.

It is like how much credit card debt you have in relation to the size of your income. The USA's credit card is almost maxed out, a precarious financial position. The ability to borrow money to pay for federal expenditures is very small.

General Valery Gerasimov Chief of the General Staff of the Armed Forces of Russia

<u>So</u> <u>a new Russian foreign policy based upon a defense of a perceived threat of aggressively</u> <u>imposed</u> <u>western values and a weakening of Russian historical power and influence</u> <u>in the</u> <u>world is developing</u>. Russia intends to reclaim its former status and respect. Remember Russia fell apart after the 1992 demise of the Soviet State and was considered to have lost the Cold War. Russia did not see itself as defeated as did the West and was humiliated by the ascendance of western influence and control. So Russia must preserve geopolitical influence on its borders and some of the former Soviet States and restore a sense of national dignity and moral high-ground. Western policy and attitudes towards Russia are in opposition to these goals and needs. There is no ideological divide as during the Cold War between Communism and Capitalism and no reason by Russia to threaten to invade Europe to occupy other countries. Yet US politicians and pundits insist upon calling Russia an existential enemy. In January 2018, the highly respected American magazine, <u>Foreign Affairs</u>, printed an article that implied Russia was now an enemy and needed to be considered as one.

The Russian Orthodox Church has resumed its former Soviet role as supporter of the Russian State (as in the pre-Communist Tsarist era going back several hundred years). Patriarch Krill is presenting the clergy as chaplains of the new empire espousing traditional Russian values of Nationalism and a Slavic State headquartered in Moscow. This includes Ukraine and Belarus. The church supports current anti-western attitudes. 80% of the Russian population identifies with the Russian Orthodox Religion. I remember when I was there in 1968 all churches were shut by the Soviet Government. This is a reversal towards the idea of Imperialist Russia. It supports a new Russian high moral ground superior to the secular consumerism of the West and its conflictive politics and extreme liberal acceptance of new social values.

To summarize: Russia's perception of the imposition of destabilizing Western political liberalism into Russia and an aggressive military NATO expansionism combined with a new US policy that considers Russia an enemy and a second-class country has resulted in new Russian defensive policies and encouraged the rise of Russian nationalism and a return to Imperialist Russian glory and international respect and influence. These policies include supporting right wing movements in Europe and the USA, advanced cyberspace capabilities, political support of Russian minorities in former Soviet Republics, rebuilding a strong modern military, and the building of a nationalistic unified state with limited managed democracy, and a strong economy. The Kremlin admits Russia is different from liberal democracies and their economic-political model is just a legitimate as that in the US, United Kingdom, or Germany. Russia is not going to duplicate them or move in that direction. Many of its citizens feel the same. I have heard them interviewed on the Internet. I thought it was interesting to hear Russian leadership say they have a tightly controlled centralized state and be very proud of that heritage. Sure, there is a western democratic liberal movement there. But it is mostly concentrated in their two main cities, Moscow and St. Petersburg, and within the more highly educated western oriented population. Go further and further from these cities and you will see a very pro-United Russia (Putin), Communist, and Nationalistic political viewpoint and party affiliation. Kind of like the USA regional split. Most of the population believes President Putin has been a great leader and brought back Russia to economic prosperity and worldwide power, prestige and influence. Go ahead ask them. I think the embedded US intellectual viewpoint about an eventual liberal Russia might just be US policy leadership kidding themselves. Maybe a Russia a little bit more flexible, but not much for a long time. And maybe a lot less flexible, especially if the West keeps pushing them. Russia is not perfect, and neither is the US. Just ask President Trump.

In a recent Wall Street Journal article dated March 18, 2018, it was stated young adults are pleased the Russian economy finally provides a variety of consumer goods and everyday freedoms the same as Europe. They believe President Putin has brought peace and stability to Russia. Many speak English. They have plans for their careers and understand the West via social media. Are they enthusiastic about political change opening up Russia as a liberal western type country? Some do, but it appears most favor the current system that offers them an optimistic future with adequate freedoms. So why risk a big change?

Countries that have successfully invaded Russia and occupied territory:

-Mongols-- 1250-1450

-Sweden-- 1600's and 1700's various years. Up to Moscow

-Poland—up to Moscow with Lithuania in 1600's, occupied Ukraine's western region.

-Turkey-won Crimean war in 1856 with French and British support.

-Japan—won Russ-Japanese war in 1905.

-France-Napoleon invasion to Moscow (but Russian Army did chase Napoleon & marched into Paris!)

-WWI-German invasion, Russian Army crumbled

-WWII-German invasion up to Moscow-30 million Russians killed

-Russian Revolution-post WWI civil war, with USA, France, British military support of the Mensheviks, the pro-western liberal provisional government opposed by the Bolsheviks-later to establish the Soviet Union. 1919-1922. See the movie Dr.Zhivago.

-The Cold War-70 years 1922-1992, with the USA and Western Europe. The Soviet Union collapsed, and the USA considered itself victorious. Russia was exhausted from an arms race with the USA and their poorly functioning economy. USA military power encircled the Soviet Union on its borders posing a dangerous threat.

--1990's-Russian economy collapses and military underfunded and demoralized, degrades into a weakened secondary power. Since 2000 country rebuilt into a major international power with a good market economy and a growing middle-class modern consumer economy similar to western Europe. National unity, pride, and security restored.

READERS NOTES: What is your opinion of Russian foreign policy? Write below.

President Putin of Russia and Steven Segal famous American action actor. Recently in 2018 Segal became a Russian-USA dual citizen and designated good will ambassador between Russia and the USA.

UKRAINE

Russian Control of Ukraine in red

Ukraine is 1400 km or 818 miles wide east to west, the distance from New York City to Chicago. It became part of the Soviet Union in 1922 until 1992. Intertwined culturally and economically with Russia. Home of two former Soviet Union Communist General Secretary leaders 1954-1983 (Nikita Khrushchev and Leonard Brezhnev). Far western Ukraine (city of Lvov) located alongside Poland became part of the Ukraine in 1945 and is the primary source of far-right wing neo-Nazi ideology and violence, anti-Russian hatred, and very influential in the new Kiev Ukraine government. This region was part of Poland from 1920-1945 and historically a European mixture of Ukrainians, Poles, Germans, Rumanians, and Jews.

It remains to be seen how the Ukrainian issue will play out. I will tell all of you this, Russia will <u>never allow Ukraine</u> to be part of NATO and aligned with the West and will never leave Crimea. These are two issues that could result in a major military conflict. Interestingly Russia has a major naval base in Sevastopol, its only domestic warm water port and it must have this for self -defense strategic purposes. Russia is also building another naval port about 200 miles (350 kilometers) east on Russian soil on the Black Sea. The world is actually safer now that Russia feels a sense of security it will not lose this critical base in Crimea on the Black Sea. Crimea also was a part of Russia for several centuries and has a substantial majority Russian population. President Khrushchev gave Crimea to Ukraine in 1953 as goodwill gift in response to Stalin's starvation of Ukraine in the 1930's. Ukraine has always been fought over and subdivided. In 1675 Poland and Russia split Ukraine. The Ottoman Empire (Turks) occupied it, and many western Ukrainians joined with Germany during WW II. The eastern Donbass and Luhansk region, about 5% of the country, for all practical purposes are now a Russian Protectorate. Russia is providing financial assistance to rebuild the country and aid after the destruction of a bloody civil war between the separatists and the Ukrainian Army. 13,000 people have been killed, mostly civilians. The currency is now in Russian Rubles and the official language is Russian. Ukraine has cut off electrical power and people's pensions in this region intermittently. Russian military forces only entered Ukraine to push back the advancing Ukrainian Army that was slowly defeating the Separatists. Now the artificial border is stable but some artillery is still exchanging fire. A compromise must be reached based on realism and not idealistic notions. In a compromise both parties are not completely happy about the result. Russia is here to stay as a world power and must be dealt with at worst as a rival with different viewpoints and history, and at best as a strategic partner solving particular world problems according to international law.

REMEMBER THIS: *Russia is called The Russian Bear*, very aggressive and powerful if provoked, and is being gradually pushed further into a corner. And if someone is waving their hands, teasing, and taking the Bear's food, sooner or later that Bear will come at you furiously and fight back. NATO, the USA, are playing with fire, creating a very risky and dangerous situation and don't even realize it. That's is what I am trying to tell you, this is a warning of what might happen under unforeseen circumstances. It appears to be happening. My Russian business lawyer friend Ilya told me Russia will never back down and knows how to suffer and survive. I believe it.

One should not be distracted by the internal policies of the Russian government which you may not agree with because they do not meet American and liberal ways of doing things. They may seem rough at times and without as much due process. You may not "approve", but it is Russia and is different from the West. This section of the book is only about the evolving Russian foreign policy point of view and the conflict with the USA and NATO.

February 14, 2014 Maidan Kiev

Here is what I have surmised since watching the 2014 Maidan in Kiev on TV in 2014, and reading numerous articles, books, TV news, and internet communications from eastern Europe and Ukraine. The Maidan was/is a very well-intentioned movement by sincere Ukrainian people for a better life, a higher standard of living, like seen in Poland, Hungary, and Germany. But Ukraine has particular problems that make this goal difficult. I admire their courage. To become more independent and economically sustainable is important. But the country is still run by special interests and has not changed much since before 2014. So go ahead and subscribe to the pro-Russian internet newsletter Slavyanka published in Canada. See the other viewpoint, it won't hurt you. Then decide what you believe. Here I saw the battle lines, pictures of combat, speeches by local leaders and Russian and Ukrainian viewpoints. Some of you will be upset with me, but this is just one viewpoint which needs to be considered and debated. Victoria Nuland, the US Assistant Secretary of State for European and Eurasian Affairs at that time and appointed by President Obama, stated publicly the US has invested over $5 billion dollars in Ukraine since 1991 for humanitarian purposes, infrastructure and to influence its government and population to become pro-western (and anti-Russian-the Orange Revolution). With this gigantic investment it's no wonder the US is trying to keep Ukraine friendly to Western Europe and NATO. They have to protect their client, so it will achieve their goals and not waste this huge sum. Wouldn't you? She is married to Robert Kagan, the major Neocon thinker who considers Russia a major military threat that must be subdued. I listened to her conversation with Geoffrey Pyatt, the US Ambassador to Ukraine in March 2014, that was widely dispersed on the internet.

VICTORIA NULAND ON PHONE WITH US AMBASSADOR TO UKRAINE PICKING NEXT INTERIM UKRAINE PRIME MINISTER AFTER FEBRUARY CHANGE IN KIEV GOVERNMENT. ARSENIY YATSENYUK IN MIDDLE WHO WAS THE US CHOICE.

At this meeting with three potential Ukrainian leaders present they discussed who would be the first interim President of Ukraine. She has high ideals but is also influenced by the ideas of the Deep State, the Neocons. She feels an obligation to promote liberal democracy everywhere the US is called or thinks it must intervene. During these violent time dissidents from western Ukraine arrived to encourage violence and an immediate change in government. In essence a revolution. I saw Ukrainian government police on fire from Molotov incendiary cocktails thrown at them from the Maidan crowd. Yes, the police fired and injured demonstrators, but they seemed primarily defensive using shields and armored vehicles to block advancing crowds, who were trying to occupy government buildings. Didn't the US military shoot and kill 20 Kent State innocent college students in 1970? Violence gets out of hand when demonstrations breakout out into riots. Large piles of tires were ignited by the demonstrators causing massive fires and chaos. Violence intensified as mercenary private armed fighters from the western Ukraine area arrived where an intense anti-Russia attitude existed. This is a region much less Russian and mostly Central European in ethnicity and culture. Yes, the police fired and hurt protestors, but the protestors had occupied government buildings and armed fighters were intermingled with the Maidan protestors. There is some good evidence that they also incited severe violence and had snipers shooting at both the Government police and the protestors to inflame conflict. Fighters: Protestors militia 12,000; Government law enforcement 8,000. Casualties: Protestors 266 killed/missing, 1,100 wounded. Government 13 killed, 339 wounded. Total civilian protestors up to 800,000.

It is complicated but in March 2014 an agreement was reached and signed between the Ukrainian government and Maidan rebels. Several European countries, Germany, France, Poland, and Russia were observers. It was to provide a compromise peace plan and hold free elections in December 2014. Peace and normal daily life was to recommence. The government was not to use its militarized police against civilians. The political status quo would remain. However, this agreement was not implemented and the Ukrainian Government at that time fled the country under duress as violence against the existing government continued to erupt with anti-Russian militia surrounding the key government buildings, rampaging through Kiev, and trying to capture the President and his staff. A new government was then voted into office by the RADA (Ukrainian Parliament) 280-0 but many members who opposed this change were not present. Others were afraid to dissent. A new government elected itself into office that was extremely anti-Russian and encouraged by the USA. Many people besides the Russian Government consider this a violent coup or forced non-democratic change of government. Shortly thereafter the Ukrainian Army invaded the eastern Donbass rebellious regions that were closely aligned with Russia and a major war began which lasted almost 2 years. At that time the US Central Intelligence Agency Director visited Kiev. Sadly, there are those who believe the US supported this questionable illegal change of government and encouraged the Ukrainian strong military response. The new Ukrainian President said the Donbass region was in for a "nasty surprise" in June 2014. The Ukrainian Army attacked the Donbass rebel-controlled region resulting in massive fighting in over 3 cities and a strategic airport. (Luhansk, Donetsk, Mariupol). The US supported this attack quietly. Russian troops were not present, perhaps only as advisors and a very small contingent of volunteers. And yes Russia eventually responded with its "voluntary militias" to push back Ukrainian military units and protect and bring peace to the unfortunate civilians in that area. Russia did not unilaterally invade Ukraine. Their security forces may have helped the Donbass rebels assert themselves and create protests against the new Ukrainian government as the US Central Intelligence Agency would do and has done as part of its mission in the world since WWII. I have seen on the internet from numerous sources, videos, photographs, and original articles and documents in detail that illustrate this civil war. I have seen a woman with a leg blown off reaching out in anguish, trying to get a cell phone to call her daughter before she died, destroyed buildings, civilians running to hide in fear as the Ukrainian artillery bombarded their own cities and citizens, seemingly to punish them and force them to submit. In Odessa a group of Russian civilians were locked in a building and burned alive by a group of Ukrainian far right militia disguised as civilians. Yes both sides created destruction, but the Ukrainian Army was the primary attacker before the Russian voluntary para-military intervened to push back the Ukrainian Army and protect the Donbass cities and people. Yes, the M-17 passenger plane shooting down incident was horrible but might have been a terrible mistake by an inexperienced untrained Donbass rebel fighting unit using a sophisticated Russian anti-aircraft weapon, "BUK radar-controlled missile launcher". At that time the Ukrainian Airforce was flying fighter jets over rebel territory and large cargo military supply aircraft. These soldiers mistook the civilian passenger plane as a military threat and fired on it. They did not know to detonate the missile before it hit the aircraft. The crew was newly trained, and the missile system is complex. The numerous internet sources I have seen convince me this is what most likely happened. No one would purposefully shoot down a civilian aircraft. Horrific collateral damage. I heard there is a video out there that seems to lend support to this point-of-view showing the BUK firing team on the radio reporting to military headquarters moments after the explosion. Was this false information? It still is also possible the Ukrainian military was involved. And how come almost no news has come out after the Dutch review of the damaged aircraft? The air traffic controller was unavailable to be interviewed. That raises questions. Ukraine had closed civilian jet airspace below 32,000 feet altitude. The plane was flying at 33,000 feet, a small margin. And that day BEFORE the incident 160 civilian passenger aircraft had flown over the Donbass just over 32,000 feet. What in the world? Why take this risk when a small 200 mile 30-minute diversion would have provided total safety from attack? I would have flown the plane myself or parachuted out. This is a good example of business putting profits ahead of passenger safety (slightly higher fuel costs for the diversion) and a culture that is always in a hurry. Very bad. The plane shouldn't have been there, and this tragedy would not have happened. The plane was shot down in the fog of war due to the airline companies' negligence. And remember if Ukraine had not invaded Donbass with the likely encouragement of the USA, this never would have happened. A real tragedy.

I have also seen numerous pictures and videos of quasi-independent Ukrainian military units from western Ukraine with Nazi swastikas and lightning bolt insignia on their uniforms which were worn by the NAZI SS Stormtrooper elite troops that reported directly to Hitler in WWII. It is a fact that many men in western Ukraine fought alongside the German Army against the Russian and Ukrainian Armies then. These two current Army Units are <u>the Right Sector in central eastern Ukraine and the Azov Battalion in Mariupol, near the Black Sea</u>. But they also favor a strong nationalistic autocratic government that is not aligned with the West and replaces the current one in Kiev. It is complicated.

NEO-NAZI UKRANIAN MILITIA

ODESSA Burning Building Pro-Russians trapped inside

I also have to tell you about the 48 Ukrainian/ Russian civilians that were locked into a government building in Odessa, Ukraine on May 2, 2014. Odessa has a large Russian population that was not in favor of the new Kiev government they considered illegitimate. For several days peaceful demonstrations were occurring which turned to violence. The pro-Russian group of civilians, women, and children ran into the building for refuge from an attacking crowd led by a right-wing Neo-Nazi paramilitary group from western Ukraine. The building was set on fire by throwing Molotov Cocktails. They surrounded the building and prevented any rescue by police or fire while these innocent people burned to death to prove a point to the population not to favor Russia. Many who tried to escape were shot or severely beaten. This is a fact. You can see this on You Tube very clearly. Molotov Cocktails (fire burning homemade bombs) were thrown into the building which started the fire. They were made by young women nearby. Go ahead, check it out. Also, it was apparent that "agent provocateurs" were present that were dressed in terror disguises pretending to be part of the pro-Russians, shooting into the Ukrainian crowd (their own people!) to provoke them into attacking the pro-Russian demonstrators and create chaos. It worked. In the video you see these disguised armed men talking with the local police, revealing their true affiliation. It illustrates their willingness to use radical violence to achieve their anti-Russian aims. This was widely disseminated in the news and not conjecture. But it has never been fully investigated by the Ukrainian nor local government and ignored by the western press. Civil wars are horrible. The "agent provocateurs" were also at the Maidan demonstrations in Kiev and instigated violence against the then existing government. They were also an integral part of the February 2014 political coup that caused the government to flee under fear of violence and ushered in the current government. The current government is highly influenced by the Svoboda Party (Freedom Party) originated in western Ukraine with many members in key political positions. It was originally named the Socialist Nationalist Party of Ukraine in 1940 and was pro-Nazi during WWII and was renamed Svoboda Party in 2004. It is the strongest far Right Wing Party in Europe and intended to banish the Russian language, although it is the primary language of 33% of Ukraine and the second language of the other 67%, and institute harsh anti-Russian laws. This includes elementary schools depicting Russia as evil and an enemy and banning all Russian movies. All statues of Lenin were destroyed, but a monument to a WWII Ukrainian Nazi leader Steven Bandera was erected in Kiev. The interim Prime Minister from February to May 2014, Arseniy Yatsenyuk, was picked by the USA foreign policy officials in Ukraine and had close ties to the Svoboda Party. He is an educated economist and lawyer who desired Ukraine to join the European Union and NATO and break all ties with Russia which he considered a continuation of the Soviet Union control of Ukraine. Interestingly, some of his family roots are traced back to Rumania, not Russia. Prior to 2012 the Svoboda Party platform included these points: Renunciation of the 2010 Kharkov Agreement that Russia's Black Sea Fleet may remain in Crimea through 2042, abolition of Crimean autonomy, nationalization of major enterprises, greater state control of the banking system, and a ban on privatization of land. Hello there! American and European capitalists, is that what you want? Holy Cow Christine LaFarge! (President of the IMF and former Finance Minister of France). And Russia? You think Russia is going to lose control and abandon its main naval base? All of this is fighting words.

Today Ukraine is still struggling to unify and almost appears to be a composition of feudal like independent regions controlled by local wealthy oligarchs, some even with their own paid militia. Although fearful and resentful of Russia, Ukraine was supported economically by Russia, and is culturally and politically similar. Most of Ukraine is not "neo-Nazi" but these influential groups fuel the flames of anti-Russian attitudes and the war against the Donbass separatists. And it makes Russia nervous.

I was raised by a Ukrainian step-father amid Ukrainian people. They were wonderful and friendly loyal Americans. My step-father, John Chubaty, used to try to imitate those Cossack dancers crouching down and kicking their legs out in front of them. It was pretty funny. The Ukrainians are great people. Now the Ukraine, Russia, and perhaps Germany and Poland need a year long peace conference just as the US and Vietnam did in 1970-73. Compromises need to be made. Ukraine cannot any longer be torn apart. The US needs to take a more passive role in this process. It is primarily a European geo-political issue. If Russia extended the war the US could intervene, if it thought very necessary.

The US also does not need to provide $1 trillion of lethal military arms to the Ukrainian Army either as proposed. The US just approved $46 million of military aid heading to the Donbass region-for sophisticated tank killer Javelin weapons and long-range sniper rifles. Total military aid to Ukraine in 2018 was $200 million and $250 million has been approved by the US Congress for 2019. That's our (USA) hard earned tax money that could be used to fund our health care system, which heals people, does not destroy and kill others. Give Ukraine some humanitarian assistance for people's pensions and rebuilding if you must help, USA Congress. Get off this warpath ideology. It is dangerous and oversimplified.

This is a war that cannot be won without a large attack backed with American soldiers and air support. This could lead to a major war as the US would be fighting directly the Russian Army. This is unacceptable. Best to accept the status quo, preserve peace, and focus on rebuilding Ukraine. This would be a massive process. The European Union has already given 7 billion dollars and is upset that Ukraine is still full of corruption and politically unstable. Russia is also owed at least $10 billion for prior assistance and natural gas. The Ukraine economy is not strong enough to repay this massive amount. Ukraine is trying to hold itself together, so it does not become a failed state. Russia could help with the rebuilding if Ukraine adopted a neutral position on the economy and militarily. Today the government sponsors a massive anti-Russian attitude among the population. Youngsters are taught to consider Russia the enemy. And to think many families have relatives in both countries. I know a woman in Moscow whose mother is Crimean. She has visited her there many times.

By the way, it is possible that the Ukrainian Army is planning to invade the Donbass Region by provoking Russia and blaming it on the Putin government. Recently in January 2018 the Ukrainian Government passed a law that the Donbass and Crimea are part of Ukraine and need to be reunited with Ukraine. Russia considered this tantamount to an act of war and denounced the law. Just possibly the USA Neocon Security Deep State and NATO might be tacitly approving this strategy. However, I think the current Trump Administration might be holding this back. As I stated much of the US Congress is in favor of giving Ukraine $1 trillion in lethal modern weapons. Can you believe it? The is the first step to create havoc in Russia and dispose of the current government and weaken the country into several regions beholden (managed) by the West. Look out below!

Note: If not outright military action then strong measures to break the Minsk II Agreement and push hard to remove Russia from the Donbass region to reintegrate it back into Ukraine, even if the Donbass people want to stay closely aligned with Russia. Currently Ukraine is intermittently shelling artillery into civilian areas to provoke and intimidate the local population and instigate a conflict. The Donbass militia retaliate to defend itself and hold the uneasy front line. Send in new independent observers to report about this artillery bombing. The ones near there now seem ineffectual and afraid to make any meaningful comments. You can see all this on YOU TUBE, from various sources.

Recently in early 2018 the Ukrainian Oligarchs were trying to suppress efforts to expose themselves as corrupt and weaken their power. According to The Economist December 17, 2017 issue, The NABU anti-corruption agency, set up by the US FBI, is under attack by Ukrainian politicians and Oligarchs that fear losing their secret illegal deals and widespread graft. Ukraine risks falling into feudal violence and becoming a failed state. Powerful men are not only measured by their wealth, but by inside political influence, private TV channels, and the size of their local private armies. Ukrainian anti-corruption measures and development of a transparent civil society with democratic values has deteriorated. The European Union has been unable to get Ukraine on a new western liberal path. Ukrainian attitudes toward Russia are slightly improving. This is playing into Vladimir Putin's strategy to regain influence over Ukraine. The American and European governments may soon lose their interest in support of the economic sanctions as Ukrainian corruption continues. I was told by a Russian businessman half-jokingly that if the US provides their promised $ 1 billion of military aid, much of it would illegally find its way to African regimes anxious to increase their military strength.

DONBASS FIGHTING SPRING 2018

UKRAINE ECONOMY and a POLITICAL SOLUTION

It remains weak although showing small improvements. Poverty remains high. The currency is weak, encouraging exports which are limited but making the cost of living higher since many consumer goods are imported. Ukraine owes Russia $3 billion for repayment of a bond issue due and has refused to repay it plus an overdue natural gas bill of at least $10 billion. The IMF (International Monetary Fund-controlled by France, Germany, United Kingdom, USA) has advanced Ukraine $6.7 billion to restructure so it can become a viable country and qualify for being a member of the European Union, and by implication, a protectorate of NATO. The total IMF commitment is $17.5 billion. This money is actually in fact a gift because Ukraine will never be able to pay it back for a long time. The repayment is Ukraine's allegiance and dependence to the West, Europe, and the USA for geo-political purposes, and of course some of the citizen's well-intentioned ideals that life would be better detached from Russia. Actually, the Russian debts should take payment precedence over the IMF debt. The IMF and the European Union have so many restrictions and stringent qualifications that Ukraine will have difficulty meeting them.

From a banker's perspective, Ukraine is a very risky investment and despite some improvement has a long way to go towards anti-corruption and privatization targets. Many of its rich oligarchs have close ties to Russia. Ukraine recently in 2018 issued 15-year Eurobonds at a 7.3% interest rate compared to .79 % for France and other similar countries. That is under 1% for 10-year money. Ukraine's bond rating is up to CA2 from CA3 according to Moody's Investment Services. That is defined as having substantial risks, worse than B bonds that are highly speculative. This is extremely risky, and I doubt the bonds have the Ukrainian land base as collateral. I would never buy them, and I was a bond portfolio manager and banker. Risk oriented private hedge funds, wealthy individuals with aggressive money looking for high yields are buying them. And Sovereign Wealth Funds (SWF) in large quantities. SWF's have increased enormously in recent years and represent surplus budget balances in various countries. It seems they might be starting to invest in too many risky assets with their nation's wealth, setting up a financial crisis. These funds are also political since they represent a countries special interests and might be used to gain economic control of another region or country. So, it makes sense that anti-Russian or pro-Ukraine, or pro-NATO countries would use these funds for geo-strategic political reasons. That may account for the large interest in buying these bonds, because Ukraine is undoubtedly a risky financial credit. So, these large institutional investors support the Ukraine's independence movement and take the risk. Would the Morgan Chase Bank or Bank of America, or large insurance company's investment portfolios or even Goldman Sachs take this risk? I don't think so. I wish the Ukraine success, but they are in a very tough place. And the bond proceeds are being used to pay down other debt. Wow. Debt to pay the IMF debt. Russia might bail them out if the two countries were realigned.

Practical Political Solution----Ukraine, the United Nations, and NATO must recognize Crimea is now in the Russian Federation. Donbass (Luhansk, Donetsk}, the Black Sea port city of Mariupol, and a pathway to Crimea along the Black Sea might possibly be granted to Russia as a Protectorate. This region severs ties with Ukraine. Far western Ukraine, the Lvov area, is granted a measure or degree of independence. This may be unrealistic. It is the creation of a quasi-independent region west of Ternopol to Poland. Still part of Ukraine but perhaps considered non-voting in the Rada with the possibility of becoming an independent country, similar to Puerto Rico in the USA. This is now being considered in the western area. Since 1600 western Ukraine has been part of Poland for much of its history even during the 20th Century prior to WWII. Lvov is only 50 miles from the Polish border and a very European city. Since 1600 western Ukraine has been occupied by Poland, Sweden, Lithuania and the Austro-

Hungary Empire, a Germanic influence. The problem is during WWII over 50,000 Poles were massacred by the Ukrainian pro-Nazi militia, which is today's Svoboda Party.

In 1931 the primary language of the population of Lvov was Polish (63%), and only 12% spoke Ukrainian. It was the 3rd largest city in Poland. Poland also tried to change the culture and make it more Polish. Ukrainians were repressed. All Ukrainian college professors were purged and dismissed. In 1918 the western Ukrainian People's Republic was formed as a revolt against Poland but was defeated militarily by Poland. Austrian Hapsburgs also had influence and invited western Ukrainians to become representatives in their government. In 1900 western Ukraine was part of the Germanic Austro-Hungarian Empire and German culture was introduced. Romania also had an influence. In 1985 The Peoples Movement of Ukraine was formed and is being reconstituted now. Its goal is to eliminate Russian influence and a resurgence of Russian control of western Ukraine. This area was instrumental in the Maidan in 2014 and has created militias with Nazi symbols to fight Russia in the Donbass today. Arseniy Yatsenyuk is from Chernivtsi in far southwestern Ukraine and was appointed by the USA as interim President from February to May of 2014. The city was part of Romania from 1918 to 1945, and also Moldavia and Romania from 1359 to 1775. In 1930 only 18% of the city was Ukrainian, another 21% German, 23% Romanian, and 27% Jewish. In April 2016 the city banned the use of the word "Russia" on billboards, advertising, and any public board. The point I am making is that this area and its people do not have a strong historical and cultural connection to Russian and eastern Ukraine. Today the city is 80% Ukrainian as other ethnic groups were forced out. Petro Poroshenko was elected President of Ukraine in May, 2014. It is interesting he is from Eastern Ukraine and is an extremely wealthy Oligarch with a huge business that makes chocolate and Russia is its main source of sales.

During WWII in 1943 the Ukrainian Resurgent Army, affiliated with Nazi Germany massacred over 25,000 Poles from Lvov. Western Ukraine was never part of the former Russian Empire. Yet this region is extremely anti-Russian. Soviet Russia eventually acquired control of this area in WWII. After the Treaty of Riga in 1921, when Soviet Russia defeated the weak Ukrainian People's Republic, near Kiev, western Ukraine was divided among Poland (controlled most of the territory), Czechoslovakia, and Austria-Hungary. Nikita Khrushchev and Leonard Brezhnev, the Russian Soviet leaders from 1954 to 1984, came from the Ukraine. Yes, it is very complex. My point is that you can see far western Ukraine was under control of central European nations and developed a connection with them and culture that was far different than Russia and eastern Ukraine. Western Ukraine effectively was part of Poland for many years and back to 1667. Today much of the Ukrainian government is influenced by western

Ukraine. Many also believe this region accelerated the Maidan peaceful demonstrations into violence and thereby motivated eastern Ukraine to rebel. Their violent militia in Kiev in February was responsible for chasing out the pro-Russian government and causing the political coup that destroyed the agreement that called for a free election in 10 months and encouraged peace. Since that time the Ukrainian government has created a country dedicated to hating Russia, banned the Russian language, and teaches small children Russia is an enemy intent on destroying Ukraine. Six million Ukrainians did perish in 1933 when Stalin cut off their food supply, but he also killed many Russians during his purges. After WWII Ukraine became an important part of the Soviet Union and contained most of their defense industry. Khrushchev gave Crimea to Ukraine in 1954 as restitution for this horror.

I think the USA has to sit down with Russia and simply ask, "Russia, what is it you want?" I don't think this simple question has been addressed face-to-face. Rather it is the EU and NATO, the US, telling Russia what it should do, how it should act, what it should believe. Naturally Russia reacts. With their concerns in hand the West can respond and seek out a compromise. Do it, now. Please.

Let's look at Ukraine's economy. Compare 2015 to 2017 statistics. GDP per capita nominal $3813 to $2165 and as PPP $15,000 to $8305. GDP from $173 billion to $92 billion. On a PPP basis** $700 billion to $336 billion. GDP growth rate 1.6% in 2018 from minus 8% in prior two years. Current industrial production is up slightly from last year. Public Debt as a % of GDP has risen from 37% to 81%. Financial foreign exchange rate from 8 to 26. (high is bad, takes more local currency to buy foreign goods). Policy short term interest rate raised to 17%. Inflation 14%. Russia is or was Ukraine's biggest trading partner at 14% of GDP.

**PPP is Purchasing Power Parity-adjusts for differences in cost of living/price level and foreign currency exchange rate adjustment

Let's look at Russia's Economy for the 2015 to 2017 period. It has suffered due to the 50% drop in world oil prices. Over 50% of their economy is exports of gas and oil. GDP: $2153 billion to $1363 billion (2.1 trillion to 1.4 trillion). A businessman told me about 30%-40% of the Russian economy is underground, that is unreported income paid in cash. That would increase their current GDP from $2.3 trillion to $3 trillion on a non-adjusted PPP basis. On a PPP basis GDP is $4 trillion the same as Germany ranked #6 in world. Or almost $5 trillion with the cash underground economy included. Now that exceeds all other European countries and places Russia #5 in the world behind China, USA, Japan, and India. The United Kingdom is $3 trillion. Russian GDP per Capita declined $15,025 to $10,240 nominal and on PPP basis from $33.000 to $28,000 now up to 31,000. The United Kingdom nominal is $44,000, South Korea $40,000, Poland $45,000, and Sweden $53,000. The current 208 Russian GDP growth rate of 1.5% is up from minus 3% (and + 7% per year from 2002-2008). Industrial Production unchanged recently 2015-2017. Public Debt as a % of GDP increased from 9.7% to 13% (very low); Policy government bank short term interest rate 8%; Inflation at 5%; Currency Exchange Rate; 31 (2014) to 64 (2019). External Debt as a % of GDP 30% to 40% in 2016. Bonds are rated BB+ (fair) and saleable in world money markets. World oil prices have rebounded to /barrel which will provide Russia an ample budget surplus to fund government operations.

NOTE: Today with the price of oil at near $60 per barrel, Russia's economy is getting a boost. When the price of oil declined from $110 to $40 Russia cut spending in both Defense and Domestic areas to balance their budget At an oil price of $55 per barrel Russia runs a balanced budget. No deficit. This type of good planning would be unlikely in the chaotic US political environment. With higher oil prices Russia can resume postponed spending with a solid balanced budget, giving the country staying power and the ability to buffer it from any imposed US economic sanctions. NOTE: As of November 5, 2018, Russia is now the WORLD'S LARGEST EXPORTER OF WHEAT. That will surprise many of you.

USA, the Big Dog: GDP per capita $59,000 in 2017. GDP now $20 trillion. Policy Federal Reserve interest rate raised from .25% to 2.25%. GDP growth rate 1.7% in 2016, at 2.4% rate for 2017-18 and now in 2019 perhaps running about 3%. Public Debt as a % of GDP 105% (high). Bonds are AAA and viewed by world markets as excellent. Unemployment rate 3.4% but does not consider low wages and reduction in labor force participation rate. Potentially high deficits due to 2018 tax reductions. Higher growth might be unsustainable.

And a little about CHINA-THE NEXT BIG DOG: China has a larger GDP now at $23 trillion on a Purchasing Power Parity basis and smaller at $15 trillion on a nominal basis compared to the US at $21. It was only $1.5 trillion in 1990. From 1993 to 2017 its economy grew at a 12.9% rate per year and a 9.4% real rate net of inflation. The USA real rate ranged from 2-4% from 1990 to 2007 and about 1.5%-2% since 2010.

At a 5% nominal growth differential (China 10%-US 5%) over 5 years China will have a nominal GDP of $22 trillion to the USA $26 trillion and exceed the USA by $12 trillion on a PPP basis ($38 trillion to $26 trillion). From the comparative viewpoint of major cities, the GDP per capita of New York City is #1 worldwide at $82,000, Moscow is $62,000 #6, Chicago and London are $60,000, and the large Chinese cities are $18,000 to $27,000. Kiev Ukraine is only $3,650.

READERS NOTES:

How do you think China's growing economy will affect the United States?

READERS NOTES:

Are you surprised China was an immense empire for over 2000 years? Does that matter today?

Do you think China's political and economic model of one strong government-no democracy-combined with building port and infrastructure around Asia and Europe will be accepted as a better political system than the USA and make these smaller countries allies of China? Does it matter if China has a larger economy than the USA and a powerful world-wide military presence?

PEOPLE'S REPUBLIC of CHINA

China's Temple of Heaven built from 1406-1420

China intends to reclaim its status as the primary East Asia power and push the US fleet out of the East and South China Seas. A return to Empire after being humiliated by Japan and Europe for the past 175 years.

CHINA EXPANSIVE EMPIRE AND COUNTRY TODAY

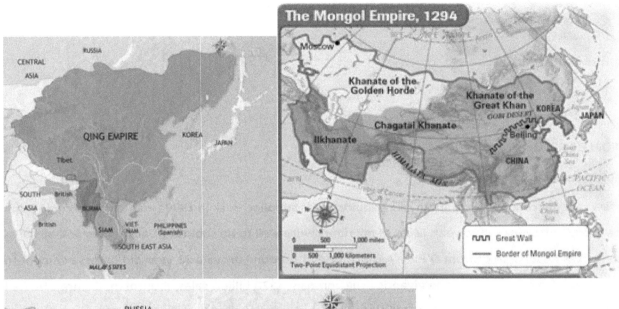

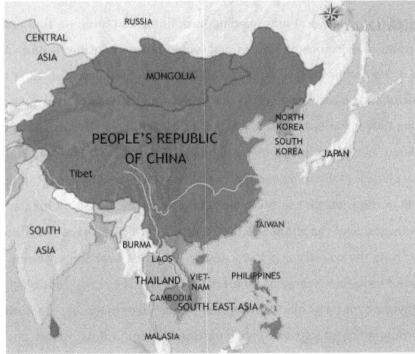

Above: Mongol Empire 1264, China Qing Dynasty 1650, People's Republic of China 2018

PEOPLE'S REPUBLIC OF CHINA

(not to be confused with Taiwan)

A few salient economic facts about our primary goods supplier. Back in 1999 I was a limousine driver in the Chicago area for over a year. Most of my riders were well to do suburban vacationers and business executives heading to or from O'Hare Airport. One afternoon I drove a 22-year-old Chinese student to the airport from Abbot Labs the gigantic drug company ($20 billion sales, Ibuprofen, Ensure). He had just finished a summer internship (MBA student) and was heading back home to China. He told me China NEVER would recognize the political existence of Taiwan and would always consider it part of China and would attempt to regain it. No compromises. So be careful everyone. He also said China's goal was to become the most powerful and largest economy in the world. And guess what, here it is, just behind the USA. On a Purchasing Power Parity basis it is just ahead of the USA (adjusted for the cost of living), $23 billion to $20 trillion. But China has so many people, 1.4 billion, with many inland who have not participated in the new Chinese globalized economy that China is way behind in per capita income, about $8000 versus $59,000 in the USA. BUT in the major Chinese coastal cities the median income is $22,000, comparable to Italy and Spain at about $25,000. China is here. They have only one political party, the Communist, that runs the country and has a strong influence over the economy. China is now a free market economy but has a high degree of government control. They call it "Socialism with Chinese Characteristics". The government owns many corporations and makes major decisions on development and finance. The government has poured MASSIVE investment in both Infrastructure and education (schools, vocational training, universities), roads, railroads, modern seaport dock loading equipment, airports, electrical transmission systems, industrial parks, roads, internet, cell phone towers, cities. This has uplifted the potential of the economy and encouraged foreign investment. Since 2000 China has spent $300 billion on education, whereas world spending is $150 billion. In 2007 they were the same at $100 billion. (source The Economist, April, 2019). China makes 50% of the world's steel and consumes 60% of world coal output. The population has a labor force that is now competitive with US and European skills. Actually, the strong Communist Party provides political stability and stable planning which allows the private free market to thrive. However, some companies and projects planned by the Chinese State fail. The second largest on-line internet consumer sales company in the world is Alibaba, behind Amazon. I have an Alibaba application on my cell phone and ordered jewelry, which was high quality and very inexpensive. The massive investment in Chinese cities and modernistic buildings "skyscrapers" is astounding. I show my students a video clip of them. Google, "10 largest Chinese Cities". All of this is made possible by huge foreign exports, an educated workforce, modern infrastructure, and foreign investment, encouraged by a stable government. China is also the world's largest producer of solar panels (and user). This is smart planning for a new Green economy unlike the USA that has strong political resistance to the idea the Green economy can produce many new jobs in a new economic sector with fossil fuels losing their necessity and dominant market position. This trend to a Green world economy is unstoppable as China's economic growth rate of 7%-12% exceeds all countries. India is second today at 7%. Despite this state planned and managed companies and projects sometimes go awry or fail. This includes some Chinese newly built planned cities that have attracted few people and business and large "Zombie" companies that are inefficient and would go out of business but are supported by substantial Chinese government subsidies to maintain employment and save the embarrassment of large losses.

In 10 years at an economic growth rate of 7% China's Gross Domestic Product will double to $46 billion. At a 2.50% growth rate the US GDP will be at $28 billion. The Chinese defense budget may then exceed the USA by $600 billion. Today the USA defense budget exceeds China by almost $500 billion. You can see why US policy makers are so concerned to raise the US growth rate. This negative growth rate differential will make it very difficult for the US to keep pace with a growing Chinese military. Today the US defense budget is $700 billion, and China is at $239 billion. This is at a US military budget that is 3.5% of GDP. If China also spends 3.5% of GDP on defense in 10 years, the US will need to increase its defense budget to 6.5% of GDP, a rate that is unsustainable and would require massive domestic spending cuts. This seems like the Soviet Union when it collapsed in 1992 trying to stay even with USA defense spending. Israel and Saudi Arabia are the only two countries with such a high rate of defense spending. Europe is in the 1-2% range. China is here to stay.

I saw President Xi Jinping on CSPAN TV speaking to a huge audience of Chinese businesspeople, officials, and foreign dignitaries. He stated in a soft confident voice about "an open and innovative China building world prosperity". That is wonderful and so cohesive. He went on that China is a truth-seeking nation with a guiding vision, that reforms itself, in which the people are the heroes of the nation. How generous, a government of the people. This is in line with ancient Confucian thought, a belief in rational moral thinking and a benevolent strong state. In the past 40 years 700 million people in China have been pulled out of poverty. He went on to say climate change is a large challenge and China is working towards green low carbon development and away from fossil fuels. And then he went on to say something I have never heard any US leader say except Native Americans, "we will treat nature with respect" What a relief and unlike my country. They will continue to target removing poverty and ease government restrictions on foreign investment and protect intellectual property rights. Business will become more transparent. Imports will be expanded to improve life for their people and tariffs reduced on foreign cars. He recognized Globalization is an irreversible trend that must be recognized and not denied or blamed on certain groups or countries. I agree. This might mean China's currency will increase in value, making imports cheaper and exports more expensive to foreign countries. He said China is not purposefully trying to create trade imbalances. This policy will reduce Chinese surpluses with countries like the USA meaning Chinese imported consumer goods will be more expensive for Americans, but China may buy more foreign goods, like American cars (Buicks are very popular there). President Trump may get his wish yet. But be mindful, this will mean less Chinese held US dollars that be will available to fund the USA budget deficits, and China may no longer be a bank funding America. I am so impressed at the way China creates long term thoughtful and sensible economic plans. This does not happen in the USA. And most of their people are happy with this and would not prefer the rough and tumble chaos of US politics and free for all market capitalism. Twelve (12) Chinese companies are also in the top 100 in the world.

China is also building a new massive 12,000 kilometer "Silk Road" from eastern China through Central Asia to Turkey north to Moscow and to Germany. Along it the Chinese are building infrastructure for themselves and these countries to encourage good relations and foreign trade. This is expanding Chinese influence and power. This will cost $900 billion and China will also invest $500 billion additional in these countries. Pakistan will receive $50 billion in new roads, bridges, wind farms, and railroads. And all of this without firing one shot. This will provide China with substantial new friendly markets for its expanding economy. Not a bad idea. There is also an ocean link (called a "Belt") going from port cities in China to Central Asia along the Indian Ocean through the Suez Canal to Greece and Italy. This is China's Road and Belt strategy to expand economic development and worldwide influence.

And now China is developing new original technology with its enhanced educational system rather than duplicating existing technology worldwide. All of these initiatives create an immense powerful Eurasian super economy led by China.

INFRASTRUCTURE-----14 Big Projects-there are many more. Many are in foreign countries. **

--$473 million: The Qinling Tunnel is the longest highway tunnel in China, more than 11 miles under Zhongnan Mountain

--$532 million: The Hainan power grid project -underwater cable connects industrial island of Hainan to mainland

--$717 million Hotan Railway connects all cities and towns of Tarin Basin

--$900 million Tianhuangping hydroelectric project-power to southeastern China

**--$1.3 billion: Baltic Pearl Project-China's foreign development project, commercial residential properties near ST. PETERSBURG, RUSSIA

--$1.7 billion: The Nanjing Metro completed in 2005 and used by 2 million people a day-717 million per year.

--$2.21 billion: Wuhan Railway Station serves fast trains at 186 mph.

--$1.9 billion: Chengdu Shuangliu Airport, 4th busiest in China, in 2015 handled 42 million passengers

--$4.5 billion: Nanhui New City, a planned city to be completed in 2020 will house 1 million people

--$6.3 billion: Xiangjiaba Dam completed in 2014. Its generators produce 30.7 Kwh of energy yearly

--$2.2 billion: Qinshan Nuclear Power Plant finished 2011. It has the most nuclear reactors of any site in the world.

**--$1.75 billion: Kigamboni Bridge in TANZANIA, 680 meters long (1/2 mile)

**--$4 billion Ethiopian-Djibouti railway in Ethiopia: links capital Addis Ababato the oceanport in Djibouti, finished 2016-trains can move at 120 km per hour or 72 mph-will speed up industrialization along the railway and increase international trade.

-$200 million: Guangzou Opera House. In China.

**--$2 billion plus for the building of the Mombasa, Kenya to Nairobi, Kenya Railroad. This has cut freight travel time from 24 hours on terrible roads to about 5 hours and increased capacity to open up the interior of the country to trade.

**-- $9 billion Greece: Since 2008 numerous projects in Greece---ports, telecommunications, energy, real estate. Greece is still in financial trouble. This is China soft worldwide power expanding, as Greece has become a leading proponent for the European Union to take a softer stance about China and work with China on new European investments. Whereas the EU considers Greece a financially delinquent country, China offered Greece a financial lifeline and treats Greece as a trusted partner. Of course, this is expanding their worldwide power as a rising empire. China is the EU's second largest trading partner at $40 billion, second to the US. China's foreign direct investment has risen from zero (0) in 2004 to $180 billion in 2016 and is rising.

 Now the Czech government is very interested in Chinese investment within their country.**new USA approved major federal projects besides road improvements—ZERO** (or close to it)

China's economic platform is State Directed Capitalism. Business is considered an arm of the Chinese State ALTHOUGH some of the corporations are privately owned. Alibaba, the Chinese Amazon competitor raised $20 billion on a New York Stock Exchange Offering. China has a $300 billion 10-year plan out to 2025 to build ten key industries into world leaders using government funds and subsidies. This includes information technology, numerical control tools and robotics, aerospace equipment, ocean engineering equipment and high-tech ships, railway equipment, energy saving vehicles or cars (lookout car companies), new materials, smart city grid technology, medical equipment and supplies, agricultural machinery, and it already is the leading manufacturer of solar panels. Education will also be directed into these areas to provide creative managerial and technical skills. This new expanding economic platform is named "Chinese wisdom and a Chinese approach to solving problems facing mankind." China is offering this as a new alternative to the USA and the Western capitalistic democratic model. China is trying to push excessive US influence out of East Asia and become the new Superpower in that region.

 It already is worldwide. This is soft power.

And infrastructure is working, building economic activity for the country. Wuhan has 11 million people and has built several subway lines and bridges which are very busy as companies in high tech invest and expand. It was paid for by debt, but that is fine since it is offset by a necessary and substantial long term productive asset. The US needs to do the same.

The US is pushing back trying to maintain political and military dominance in this region far far away from America. How foolish. The US can maintain a presence without considering China a rival or worse yet, a potential enemy. Does China have a military presence near Cuba, Venezuela, and Nicaragua all Communist or socialist states with an adversarial relationship to the USA? Goodness Gracious, as Secretary of Defense Donald Rumsfeld used to exclaim.

EDUCATION in CHINA

China has invested a tremendous amount expanding and improving their educational system in the last 16 years since 2002. This includes higher education. One in five students go on to higher education. But remember this statistic includes the 1 billion population mostly in the western China provinces that have not participated in the new Chinese world. There are 37 million students enrolled in higher education. In the past 15 years China has increased the number of universities from 1022 to 2824. They have set an ambitious goal to have 40 world class universities by 2025. Seems very ambitious but the intent is there. China has 5 universities listed in the top 1% of most cited papers in math/science.

Since they now have only one university ranked as world class and two more in the top 100 there is still a long way to go. The Chinese government directs this development and has schools categorized for different levels of excellence and reputation for worldwide advanced study. In 2016 440,000 foreign students were enrolled versus 55,000 in 2006. Forty per cent (40%) of the graduates are in the STEM category, science, technology, engineering, math. This will build a strong advanced Chinese economy. The goal is to create an innovative society by 2022. China's 5-year plan now emphasizes both quality and entrepreneurship. It seeks to develop high tech skills and creativity. China calls this soft power. You can see what a highly structured economy and government can do to direct its resources towards national goals. And it has a long-range plan. The US has no such plans. It is ad hoc, let the market determine outcomes. This is part of the new Chinese model they are exporting to developing countries around the world. One does not need a chaotic and everchanging complex democratic society to achieve productive goals that improve standards of living and international power. Underneath these government mandates and plans a free market is allowed to exist and compete around the world. This is called Socialism with Chinese Characteristics. Now China is changing its emphasis from exports to more and better internal consumption to improve living standards. It is now moving upmarket to generate highly educated people who can compete creating and building products with original ideas. China has been known for using vast pools of semi-skilled workers at low wages to mass build foreign products, like Apple cell phones, or car parts, toys, ceiling fans, and many household goods.

They will soon have the educated workforce to create their own products that are competitive worldwide. This will put competitive pressure on managers and professionals in the USA, and more competition on US Corporations. (lower profits, lower compensation, less market domination). So all I can say is: "here comes China again". They will continue to build a powerful economy and country. My daughter's large high-tech American company, Motorola Information Systems, has already started hiring Chinese managers rather than sending Americans overseas to run their Asian subsidiaries. The US still has one of the best higher educational systems in the world and many leading outstanding research universities and is ranked overall with Sweden and Finland at the top worldwide. Russia is also highly rated with many graduates in STEM (science, technology, engineering, math). China is making large advances to catch up. In K-12 the US has slipped to about 17th overall and 27th in math worldwide. Russia is rated 13th. In higher education Russia has been ranked # 4 - # 10. China has just become rated in standard testing 10-11th grade, in its primary commercial cities, connected to the world economy. Shanghai and Hong Kong are ranked #1 and #2 in the world. Away from the major city's rankings are somewhat lower. The point is that China is making great strides in education and investing tremendous amounts of government funds with a long term sensible ambitious plan. Chinese students studying overseas has increased from 200,000 in 2002 to 800,000 in 2016.

New infrastructure billion-dollar bridge

Shanghai Business Center

WAR-WHAT IS GOOD FOR!

CONFLICT BETWEEN USA, RUSSIA, AND CHINA

REMEMBER THAT SONG FROM 1969? EDWIN STAR?

It's happening again. The USA is building up a head of steam about having enemies, an emotional cry to rally the American people into another conflict. After the Vietnam War my confidence in the American Government was broken and never has entirely healed.

CONFLICT SUMMARY:

-The US will be fighting on another country's homeland.

-Russia and China have the technology to shoot down US aircraft, missiles, and ships.

-Conflicts will be over very quickly and violent.

-There will be no major land war, but regional missile confrontations.

-Soft power and hybrid wars will be the form of competitive conflict over a long time period. The US is losing worldwide respect and influence due to a flawed foreign policy and overconfidence in liberal democracy and military intervention.

The USA cannot "win" any type of regional military conflict because it cannot accept ANY casualties in its naval fleet or any land forces that would be sustained from China/Russia along their sea and land borders from advanced electronic missiles and submarines. These countries are defending their homeland with defensive aggressive behavior as they have been invaded several times since 1850. They are asserting their long history as a powerful respected empire. The US military's new plan to fight two large land wars against them at the same time seems strategically unsound because todays weapon systems will cause wars to end quickly and violently. Russia and China have prepared to fight "Grey Wars" with limited military activity to offset the USA's huge advantage in force size and massive weaponry. <u>The space war race is the most important and critical military strategy.</u>

From 1991-2008 the US fought a long-protracted military conflict against both Iraq and disparate factions within the country. This included enforcement of a no-fly zone and very harsh economic sanctions imposed by the USA from 1992-2003. The Afghanistan conflict is 18 years old. Now we have conflicts against both ISIS and Syria and here we go again. And now Russia is in there, with a very powerful well-trained military, modern advanced weapons, and a very shrewd government and military. And the Russian economy isn't all that bad either, growing again with very little government debt unlike the USA, Europe, Japan, and even China. Its defense budget is 10% of the US, but they are holding several high cards and I think have the advantage should the type of war break out that is most likely. The same for China. Get in a shooting match along the vast Chinese coastline and the US will head back east minus a few ships. The American people will be outraged and fearful. US Admirals will not tolerate the US 7th Fleet ships being picked off one by one . Russia and China both have a large number of effective land to sea missiles. A huge terrible mutual onslaught would begin in this type of coastal conflict and end in a very few days. The US will declare an armistice and withdraw. China will then occupy Taiwan, their avowed goal. US worldwide influence will drastically decline. Remember for the USA a tie is a terrible loss. US invincibility will vanish overnight. Many Russian missiles are <u>on mobile flatbed truck launchers and hard to detect</u>. Think about it.

Unfortunately, there now exists a short window of opportunity until the 2020 USA election for both Russia and China to take aggressive military action. Currently the US is severely divided and in political chaos. It has an executive branch that has favorable attitudes about both China and Russia despite all the US hardline boisterous loud talk, it does not seem to consider these two countries oppositional or existential enemies. Russia could drive its military forces to Kiev, Ukraine, easily defeating the retreating Ukraine Army under the pretext of bringing stability to the Ukraine and preventing a Ukraine attack against the Donbass. China could provoke an invasion of Taiwan to finally reunify the country to the Peoples Republic of China. I believe the USA and NATO would be stunned and frozen, unable to summon the will to support a military defensive counterattack. Perhaps a minor amount of military force would try to resist the Chinese and Russian advances. But it would over very fast and become a fait accompli. <u>Once the territory is occupied it would be almost impossible to force the Chinese and Russian forces to leave without creating an enormous regional war. President Trump and the current Congress would never do it.</u> However, if the liberal Democrats were elected and controlled both Congress and the Executive Branch the US would much more likely respond with a tremendous show of military force. Remember they are the idealists, who believe in the USA as the exceptional country with the responsibility to protect the world from aggression. They believe in Russia and China as existential enemies and incorporate many of the DEEP STATE ideas in their worldview. I also believe many of them vastly underestimate the effectiveness of opposing military forces and would tend to be overconfident, leading to a disaster. I'm not recommending Russia and China occupy Ukraine and Taiwan, but this looks like the time to do it. And the US is moving rapidly to improve its ship anti-missile electronic defense system. Now that type of defense cannot substantially stop a massive missile attack. Hmmm. what do you think? And while all this is going on the Pentagon is recreating a military capable of fighting two protracted massive land wars that will never happen.

A Few Local Wars & Defense of Freedom?

The US arranged for the destruction of the Libyan government and the country's infrastructure for no valid major reason. Omar Khadhafi, their autocratic leader, was having civilian unrest violence problems with rebels and it looked grim for the rebels so now here comes the US, France, and Great Britain to the rescue with massive bombing. Khaddaffi had been hostile to Europe in the past but not at this time. The country has been destroyed and now has waring tribal and political factions. Looks like a failed state to me. And what for? Libya was no threat to NATO. In fact, it wanted good relations. But they were trying to build a united North African Confederation to create a regional power political base, to present a united front and enhance trade. Libya also has considerable oil. What started out as a geographically small specific air force military mission to stop a perceived massacre of rebel soldiers and civilians quickly became a deliberate destruction of the Libyan Government with widespread destruction far away from the rebel conflict areas.

 Victoria Nuland, State Department Spokesperson (an official title) during the Obama Administration, is now Chief Executive of the Center for a New American Security, a Washington well intentioned professional think tank started in 2007, that considers itself bipartisan. Not so sure about that. But CNAS seems to cling onto a Neo-Conservative (Deep State?) viewpoint that US worldwide country intervention is a necessary strategy and may include military action. The stated mission is to "develop strong, pragmatic, and principled national security and defense policies that promote and protect American interests and values" (around the world). Sounds OK, but it does not seem like it is thinking out of the box. Former high-ranking Commander of the U.S. Central Command General David Petraeus remarked "CNAS has in a few years established itself as a true force in think tank and policy-making circles". It includes many high-ranking US former officials including former CIA Directors, State Department officials, and academic professors. Also, several advisors to Vice-President Biden, including a former Deputy National Security Advisor to the Vice-President 2015-2017, and a senior advisor to the former National Security Advisor 2013-2015.

Madeleine Albright, Secretary of State during the Clinton period, is a member. From 1992 to 2003 the US and NATO instituted harsh sanctions against Iraq. In 1996 the Secretary was interviewed by the respected journalist Leslie Stahl on 60 Minutes on national US television. The US had severe embargo/sanctions on Iraq. Stahl: (Questioning US sanctions) "We have heard that 500,00 Iraqi children have died (567,000). I mean that's more children that died at Hiroshima. And you know, was the price worth it?"

Secretary: "I think this is a very hard choice, but the price was worth it" 60 Minutes (national television show-- 5/12/96).

Iraq Desert Storm in 1990 was not a nationalistic war supported by the Iraqi people. There was no widespread support of the continuing Iraq government after 1991. As for corruption disrupting the medical and food aid, which was insufficient, the point is that without the sanctions, except for military weapons, the population would not have undergone this suffering in the first place. It was the unnecessary sanctions, not corruption, that caused this national catastrophe. Another example of US policy run amuck and causing harmful unintended consequences. The USA must be held accountable as it demands other countries do for their human rights violations.

Also remember the USA B52 carpet bombing of Vietnamese civilians from 1967-1973 in Hanoi? Two million civilians were killed and countless others terrified. The people built "spider holes" in the cities. These were numerous miniature air raid shelters in which a person could easily pop open a cover in the ground and jump down inside a shallow hole and close the top and hide from the bombing devastation. The bombing was not limited to military and infrastructure targets. There was Operation Rolling Thunder under President Lyndon Johnson and Nixon's 1973 Christmas bombing of North Vietnam cities to convince Vietnamese leaders at peace talks in Paris to accept a war ending proposal. It sure seems like war crimes, or at least actions not befitting a spiritual Christian nation. The US dropped more tons of bombs on Vietnam and Laos along the Ho Chi Minh Trail than on all of Europe during WWII. Also, there was Hiroshima and Nagasaki, the 1945 firebombing of Tokyo civilian areas directed by General Curtis LeMay, and the firebombing of Dresden Germany during WW II (no military target-only civilian destruction to break the will of the German civilian population)> All senseless. I believe General LeMay was in favor of the USA bombing and invading Cuba in 1962 during the Missile Crisis. That could have set off a nuclear war. And how about the 78-day bombing of Belgrade, Serbia, in 1999 destroying the city and killing countless civilians? Yes, the Serbian Army was destroying the Muslim population in Kosovo and had to be stopped. But the Kosovo Liberation Army forces also inflicted damage on Serbs in their attempt to create an independent Kosovo state. OK. But why inflict such horror on innocent civilians, just because you can? Why not stick to military targets and some isolated infrastructure? This is my definition of genocidal aggression, maybe war crimes. Besides the government, Russian citizens I know still hold this against the USA. Remember, Serbia has been a Russian Ally since before WWI. A Serbian assassin killed the Austrian Archduke Ferdinand which brought in Russia to protect Serbia and was one factor that began WWI. Here is the result of the NATO bombing of Belgrade. This was part of a "humanitarian intervention" to protect Kosovo from Serbian ethnic cleansing. NATO sent 2,300 cruise missiles at 990 targets, dropped 14,000 bombs, including long lasting depleted uranium bombs, and anti-personnel cluster bombs which continue to explode and still kill and maim civilians. Over 2,000 civilians were killed, thousands injured, and the entire country terrified daily for 3 months. Airstrikes destroyed 300 schools, libraries, and 20 hospitals, 40,000 homes, and 90 historic monuments. A civilian passenger train was bombed while crossing a bridge killing 25 people on April 12, 1999. Amnesty International accused NATO of War Crimes. This bombing was outright cruel and unnecessary and shameful and cannot casually be referred to as "collateral damage". The US could have used its land forces, the Marines, to invade Kosovo to drive out the Serbian Army without resorting to massive civilian bombing. But, that might have inflicted to much harm to the US and NATO armed forces. What are they for anyway?

Hmmm...The Iraq sanctions sound like genocide to me and a war crime (and maybe the other actions just mentioned from the past). What do you think? Research Iraq. Go ahead. The problem is these types of beliefs circulate and then become "normal". They are justified by Washington think tanks with fancy names like the Center for a New American Security, Foreign Affairs magazine, Council of Foreign Relations (I was a junior social member in 1981 in Chicago), American Enterprise Institute, Atlantic Council, and many others.

They consist of key members that were and still are supporters of aggressive American foreign policy (commonly called "hawks" by the media and those opposed to their ideas). It also includes the idea that America has the right to intervene in foreign countries to promote democracy, western values, and US interests seemingly without taking into account those countries unique historical characteristics. This is an example of American thinking by many US leaders. It is disconcerting and unsettling that very highly educated persons with distinguished careers in public service would hold onto these militaristic and harsh ideas so tightly. Perhaps a new realistic and safer foreign policy paradigm is needed. These policies often have terrible unintended consequences and do not promote a safer world.

Defense Priorities Foundation is a newly established think tank that offers a counterview, that USA foreign policy should have a restrained cautious approach and a much greater reluctance to use military force and avoid foreign interventionism. It was founded by colleagues who agree with RAND PAUL, the Kentucky Republican Senator. Financially it is funded by the conservative leaning Koch Brothers, who also fund the Cato Institute. Their thinking is that the military must be used carefully and only to support a USA Grand Strategy emphasizing diplomacy and free trade. Every foreign conflict cannot be labeled an imminent threat. On July 4, 1821, John Quincy Adams, Secretary of State of the USA, and soon to become President, stated "She (the USA) Goes Not Abroad in Search of Monsters to Destroy"

By the way the USA has 7,000 MILITARY DRONES, Defense and CIA combined, just to let you know. And during 2017 had 149 Special Operations "lily pad" military sites operational at various dates. That is 75% of the world's countries. The cost: about $25 billion. On any given day special operation troops are active in 88 countries.

USA Reaper Drone

Now BACK to RUSSIA AND CHINA and the United States. Now the fun begins. CONFLICT

The USA is up against two reemerging powerful nationalistic empires with histories going back centuries to 850 AD (Russia) and 221 BC (China). Both have been invaded numerous times by "Western Forces" and suffered extensive destruction and also political and economic domination, especially China (Gunboat Diplomacy 1850-1911). This explains their nationalistic concerns and emphasis on a strong defensive military posture today.

By contrast the US is a "new empire" with only a 230-year history. Only since 1945 and the defeat of Germany and Japan has the US empire substantially grown to its enormous size and power, and respected world leadership. Today it is still searching for its identity and role as an international power. The US has been determined to spread western liberal values of democracy, individualism, freedom, and capitalism upon which the country was founded in 1776. This is distinctly different from its two rival empires, who have been autocratic centralized states, that emphasized a collective approach to society and government and whose people considered the state as a protector from hostile outside forces. Within these structures economies existed that had various degrees of market freedom and foreign trade, but usually mostly benefited the ruling elite and aristocracy.

READERS NOTES:

Should the USA reduce several of its large foreign bases to save budget dollars and consolidate its military forces to a more defensive posture? Why?

US B2 Stealth Bomber

RUSSIAN CONFLICT

Vladimir Putin, the President of Russia stated in 2012, "Those who want to return to the Soviet era have no head, and those who don't have no heart". He also has stated the worst geo-political catastrophe of the 20th Century (for Russia at least) was the dissolution of the Soviet Union. Think of that. The Soviet Union lost about 50% of its population (in 1989 it was 287 million, Russia was 147 million - now 142 million). About 25 million ethnic Russians were stranded or left behind. It was not easy to move back to Russia and give up everything in your life in former Soviet States. Eight million were in the Ukraine and now three million are in the USA. I know some in Albuquerque. I enjoy their directness and sense of humor.

The US military is changing its primary structure to be capable of fighting two large land wars at the same time against Russia and China with less assets for terrorism conflicts. These land wars will never happen. The USA has <u>already lost the improbable large land-air war to both China and Russia. And a smaller intense regional one too, as of right now, May 20, 2019</u>. Checkmate, the Russians are good chess players.

Russian Iskandar missile mobile launcher

What in the world am I talking about? Am I crazy? Just this-I didn't say cyberwar. It's a large land war, what our military is now planning for. An enlarged force capable of fighting two major extended wars at the same time. Pretty expensive for a country financially strapped (USA).

NOTE: On October 22, 2018, the Trump Administration announced it was cancelling the IBN Treaty negotiated in 1986 between the US and Russia/Soviet Union and the US will enhance its nuclear strength until Russia comes to the negotiating table with a humble conciliatory attitude. Rubbing more salt into Russia's wounds. Bad bad idea. This is potentially dangerous and destabilizing. One might say reckless. This Treaty provided for a reduction in offensive missiles, inspections, and a prohibition of land-based cruise missiles with a range from 500 km (300 miles) to 2000 km (1350 miles). Now Russian missiles will be allowed to reach all of Europe and the Middle East from scattered hard to detect sites across the vast Russian country west of Moscow. This further divides the countries and can foster mutual distrust and fear which are the basis for conflict. The Treaty allowed sea and air fired missiles which the US has used all over the Middle East since Operation Desert Storm in 1990. This put Russia at a strategic disadvantage. Serious negotiation to update this treaty would be a better solution. November 27, 2018: Conflict in Sea of Azov between Russian and Ukraine naval ships (2 old slightly updated frigates from the US Coast Guard). Russia captures the ships-detains them. Perhaps Ukraine is provoking Russia into military action to win support of USA/NATO for push back on Crimea and Donbass, where Artillery firing continues daily. Russia says Ukraine is the aggressor, could it be? Ukraine is determined to get back these regions. Even now, May 20th, 2019, the newly elected Ukrainian President proclaimed that Crimea and the Donbass must be returned to Ukraine. There is no possibility of that ever happening. July, 2019: Russia also withdraws form the INF Treaty allowing it unlimited access to build and deploy cruise missiles of any range. Compliance inspections are terminated.

READERS NOTES:

Why is Europe afraid of Russia? Sweden, not on Russia's border, is very concerned and preparing for conflict.

Look at these two maps of Chinese and Russian defensive capabilities (The Economist, January 27, 2018 & US Department of Defense). These defensive zones are named anti-access/area denial zones.

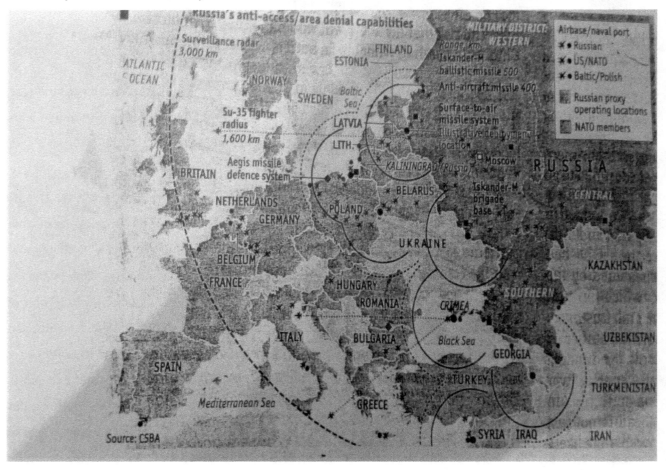

Russian anti-access denial military defense over Europe-source US Department of Defense and The Economist

The SU-400 anti-aircraft anti-missile is state-of-the-art and considered extremely effective with a radar

detection range of 373 miles.

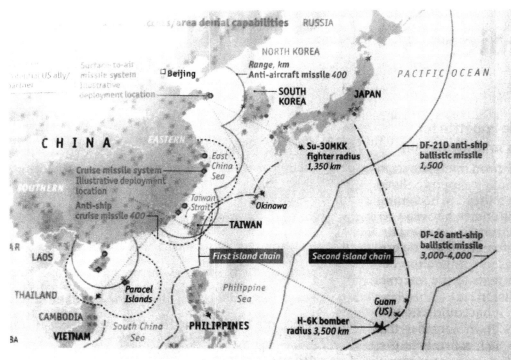

Chinese anti-access denial defense area-source US Dept of Defense, The Economist

CHINA--RUSSIAN MISSILE DEFENSE

So belligerent military forces enter at your own risk. In Europe you can see numerous Russian Intermediate Range Iskandar Missile sites (capable of carrying nuclear weapons) with a range of 500 km or 300 miles. This perimeter reaches Helsinki Finland, Stockholm Sweden, Poland, Ukraine, the Baltic countries, and most of Turkey. Syria is also encircled and protected by this system (it has the SU-200 but is being upgraded to the SU-300-400 BUK which is much more accurate and effective). Interestingly, Hungary, Romania, and Bulgaria are not within range of this missile, which is both offensive and defensive. These three European countries are more positive and less concerned about Russia as a hostile country. And just west of Russia is Serbia with very close historical-cultural ties to Russia. Both use the Cyrillic alphabet and have a similar Eastern Orthodox Rite religion. The Russian and Syrian borders are also protected by the SU-400 BUK anti-aircraft system which is considered the most capable and lethal long-range air defense missile system on the planet (RT), and highly respected by the US with a range of 150 miles. Iran also has this system. Russia also has an advanced radar system extending west to the United Kingdom and the west coast of France. Russia also is updating its small coastal surface navy consisting mostly of corvettes and frigates with short range ship to ship electronic missile capability. Twenty more are scheduled to be put into service by 2020. With the exception of its several ICBM submarines, most of its fleet are attack submarines with a variety of conventional weapons capable of destroying submarines, surface ships, and land targets. Russia has 67 submarines and the US only 71. The Russian attack submarines are focused on protecting the ICBM submarines at sea and the coastlines and are being designed to sink ships and protect the homeland. Their many small naval corvettes, frigates and destroyers are agile and quick with electronic equipment and missiles to attack naval ships. While some are old, by 2020 thirty (30) new ships and submarines will be have been added to Russia's Black Sea Fleet. They also have sophisticated new cruise missiles that were launched from naval vessels in the Caspian Sea into Syria, a distance of 1300 km or 780 miles. The INF Treaty eliminated cruise missiles with a range over 500 km or 300 miles, but exempted cruise missiles fired from sea or air. That is one reason Russia fired its missiles from the landlocked Caspian Sea. The cruise missiles that have been used since 1990 in the Middle East wars by the US have been sea and air launched, avoiding this limitation. Now Russia is building missiles that exceed this distance but are ground fired because it does not have extensive naval launch capability, and therefore may violate the INF Treaty signed by the USA and Russia in 1986 limiting distance, research, and deployment on land for advanced cruise missiles. With the Trump Administration abrogating the INF Treaty Russia is now free to build and place long range cruise missiles anywhere up to their border threatening ALL of Europe. President George W. Bush pulled the USA out of the ABM Treaty in 2002, so to some extent this is a Russian necessary defensive response. The US has put controversial anti-ballistic missiles into Poland and Romania of late saying they are to stop Iranian missiles which seems disingenuous. Rather they are meant to stop Russian long range nuclear missiles that could be fired at the USA and Europe. But this upsets the balance of power as one side feels vulnerable (Russia). Russia does not have an anti-nuclear long-range

ICBM defense system as it complied with the Treaty. This is one reason for what appears to be a very aggressive Russian military buildup, their concerns over being attacked or intimidated into submission. I think it makes a lot of sense. And it gets real complicated.

There are about 200,000 well trained Russian troops stationed near the Russian border from the Baltics to Ukraine within 48 hours of deployment to the border. They have a new Order of Battle configuration with many units at the Battalion and Regimental level (700-2500 troops) under independent operation, for quick deployment and flexibility, rather than being put together into large Divisions under central command with up to 13,000 at this level and often unwieldy and slow to respond. Russian soldiers training has been upgraded with the large draftee troops held in the rear. Estimates vary but Russia has about 75,000-100,000 extremely well-trained troops with new updated equipment similar to the US Army. They have undergone numerous military exercises the past 5 years. This is enough to fight short lived regional ground battles in today's military environment. Ok, what am I saying is that US ground forces would be eliminated before they landed by Russian ground fire and electronic radar guided missiles. Those on the ground would be hit by a massive wave of missiles and rocket fire. This is not like the Iraq war when the US had months to amass a huge ground force of 500,000 in 1990 and 150,000 in 2003. This regional conflict would be over in 3 weeks or less. Of course, US air power would cause damage but would face overwhelming defensive Russian firepower. Remember Russia would be on its homeland and be inspired to fight for Mother Russia. And Russia's electronically directed land cruise missile and nimble small missile armed frigates would sink a few American expensive ships which would be exposed out at sea. The Russian assault submarines would also play a part firing at both the US Naval fleet and any remaining ground positions near the Russian border in Donbass or even central Ukraine. Remember even older submarines can do much damage and harass and upset the battle plans of large modern fleets.

The American people will not tolerate these losses for some kind of idealistic controversial faraway war. And I think the US military would withdraw, concerned about worsening extensive losses and humiliation.

And Russia now has new highly sophisticated nuclear-powered attack submarines, the Yasen Class. Currently two are in operation with five more scheduled to be in operation starting from 2019 to 2023. They have land-attack, anti-ship, and anti-submarine missiles and torpedoes with advanced sonar with stealth movement characteristics. Hard to detect. The US has 13 Virginia Class submarines that are similar to the Yasen Class. They are slightly faster but cannot dive as deeply. Now remember it only takes one submarine to sink another American or Ukrainian submarine, a ship, or an aircraft carrier, or a land military installation. The idea in a limited conflict is to inflict just enough damage to the enemy so it stops fighting and pulls back. You do not need to destroy an enemy's fleet to win a Grey War or a limited regional conflict. This is not WWII in the Pacific with the US destroying the Japanese Navy at the Battle of Midway and the Battle of the Coral Sea. A few big hits on a few US warships and land forces will be enough for the US to cease hostilities and look for a political geo-strategic solution. Believe me. Fighting Russia or China directly or through an intense proxy war will not be any fun or a glorious mission. To put this in simpler language, the Russian armed forces are "good enough" to cause significant damage. Numerous mobile Russian Corvette electronic missile radar ships are stationed on the Black Sea. As I have stated Russia is building 20 more naval ships for its Black sea Fleet including 4 new submarines.

Russian Submarine

Russian Guided Missile Frigate

The Ukrainian Rada passed a law on January 8, 2018 that states both Crimea and the Donbass are illegally occupied by Russia and must be returned. Russia has called this an act of war. It is getting

obvious that Ukraine intends to invade the Donbass to drive Russia out with US backing. This US involvement would consist of some military hardware, intelligence, advisors and special forces to accomplish tactical quick missions. These assets are already in the Ukraine. Recently Ukraine received $46 million of military hardware from the US, Javelin anti-tank electronically guided rockets and advanced high-powered sniper rifles. These are very effective and will help Ukraine offset Russian armored units. Here goes the US again--getting involved in a proxy war in a quiet way mostly unobserved by the US media and American public. It won't matter that much because Russia, if sufficiently provoked, will smash the Ukrainian Army in three weeks if it unleashes its military power stationed close to eastern Ukraine. Remember in 2014 Russia just put in a small counter offensive force to stop the advancing Ukrainian Army to a standstill, not a defeat. This will cause the Ukrainian government to collapse and chaos will prevail over the country as different groups struggle for power. This will be a perfect time for Russia to take control and bring peace and order to the country. The US will have managed to turn Ukraine back to Russia in an attempt to save it, rather than encourage Ukraine to accept the fact Crimea and the Donbass are part of Russia and adjust to it, still intact with 90% of its territory.

A worse case is that Russia has to retreat back into Russia and is followed by an attacking Ukrainian Army supported by a small NATO backup auxiliary force. Feeling a major threat to the integrity of its border Russia will respond with a withering attack of airpower and missiles inflaming this war and causing huge NATO casualties. If that doesn't stop NATO then Russia will use tactical nuclear weapons and "small nukes", possibly 3% the size of Hiroshima, on military facilities all over Ukraine and maybe even Poland, the Baltic countries, including civilian infrastructure like power plants, bridges, and manufacturing zones. But this will never happen because Russia will stop NATO in its tracks, destroying the Ukraine Army, and Ukraine will collapse. It may also create another military incident in Latvia encouraging Russia intervention in that country. One-third- (1/3)-of the population is of Russian origin with plenty of gripes against the ethnic Latvians. It might make a good member of a newly expanded Russian Federation. Yes, the Russians will lose many troops and equipment in the Ukraine if retreating. But this will be an invasion of Russia and rally all the Russian people behind the government. And what about other countries. Will Germany support this? Hungary? Italy? Greece? France? And how about China?

THE GREY ZONE---HYBRID WAR

This is a type of limited military resolution that Russia has developed to achieve success in conflict zones. It is a combination of soft power and light military intervention. I have discussed it earlier in this book. It combines cyber interruption hacking, social media commentaries to influence foreign country attitudes and enhance political divisions, stirring up local populations to actions supportive of Russian interests, sponsoring political parties and groups with favorable attitudes towards the Russian Government, and lastly the use of limited military power. That is why Russia does not require a large standing army to be effective, although it does have about 400,000 ground troops. This war includes the use of contract and voluntary troops, limited combat, support of local rebellions, and intimidation by the presence of nearby large military units on alert, including aircraft fly by missions near opposition countries and naval ships, and large military practice exercises that can be interpreted as threatening. It also includes rallying the Russian population to support these conflicts, their government, and see other countries and NATO as aggressive threats to Russia. Also, the cultivation of influential people in opposition countries to adopt opinions that support Russia. Russia might develop close ties with US political leaders, think tanks, intelligence officers, media news people, and professors and writers to influence their thinking and get inside information about American decision makers viewpoints of Russian policies using Oligarchs connected to the Kremlin and highly trained SVR diplomatic personnel assigned overseas to Russian embassies making influential connections. The goal is not to develop foreign agents, but positive casual non-secretive relationships. Just like a US corporate lobbyist does with Congress. I read that now Russia has doubled the number of security personnel in the US since the Soviet era, to about 2,000 agents and support staff. Remember a cultural attaché means a person working within the Security Services. This strategy is also about Russia presenting itself and its political and economic model to the world to build relationships with other countries. Sounds like an effective method to me. And it's cheap. Costs much less then building and supporting a large worldwide military force and presence that gets into serious military conflicts. The Grey Zone conflict strategy is to create ambiguity to leave regions unsure how to respond militarily. It is stealth like in that there is no clear noticeable beginning, no announcement, as it spreads misinformation and propaganda and influences regional governments. There is electronic disruption of military command and control functions. Russia can use this in a military conflict. These strategies can be justified as protecting local populations. Russia becomes the liberating hero. In fact, it just might be. Their long run strategy is stop former Soviet border states from becoming under the influence of the West and connected by Treaty. Interference in other countries via cyber tactics and financial support of nationalistic political groups creates a favorable environment to the resurrection of the Russian nationalistic state (and historical empire). And these conflicts can be protracted, with the goal of just destabilizing over a prolonged period (Georgia, Ukraine, potentially Latvia). War in the Gray Zone does not need a clear-cut winner to achieve its purpose.

A somewhat similar strategy is developing within China: cyber intervention, world-wide foreign country economic investment with surplus reserves from exports, introducing the Chinese model of a centralized and single party-political system managing a market economy with strong government long range planning, "State Directed Capitalism". This is the Chinese political and economic platform. It does not include ideas about liberal democracy and individualistic freedom. It just works and is easier to manage without the chaos and intermittent upheavals in a liberal democracy. More harmonious. And building prosperity and prestige for the Chinese people. For over 2000 years the ancient philosophy of Confucianism has permeated China to this day. This is a harmonious cooperative society based upon an accepted moral code and managed by a large powerful bureaucratic state or empire. This is the very definition of the Chinese Communist Party. The US has many complex situations to manage. Wow! A direct conflict with a clear win-lose ending would be simpler and easier to solve. Then the powerful US military juggernaut would be very effective. There really are no such wars anymore. Look how Iraq became an expensive protracted insurgent urban conflict. The US forces could not identify the opposing force that often blended into the population. Afghanistan has been an 18-year stalemate of US intervention with no defining goals having been achieved. What to do in Afghanistan? Who knows because the US military, intelligence services, Congress, and executive branch Asian experts surely do not know. I do not believe the Taliban is a direct threat to the USA and withdrawing would not increase terrorism in the USA or Europe. Warlords and a corrupt government and the Taliban currently control the country. More money and lives wasted for what?

It's a bad situation with no immediate good answer. One proposed is to stay there indefinitely, continue a low grade destabilizing war. Really? The US has some tough decisions ahead in foreign military policy.

MILITARY CONFLICT WITH CHINA

China has already won just like Russia. so why start one?

Chinese aircraft carrier. Only one in fleet but more being planned.

DF-21D Chinese Carrier Killer Cruise Missile

China is in the same historical position as Russia, resurrecting its ancient empire and adapting it to modern times. It also melding their idea of Communism with a worldwide economy that generates wealth. China calls it "Socialism with Chinese Characteristics" One might add with military strength and international respect and admiration. They are progressing along this path. Oh, and just like Russia, China's internal method of governing does not agree with some western values and is highly disciplined, perhaps harsh. But it is not the USA's role to criticize China and try to change it, as the Obama Administration did. China is pushing back hard against US influence in Asia.

Since 221 BC China has experienced 23 dynasties. That is over 2200 years ago. The first, the Qin, built The Great Wall and the awesome Terra Cotta Army Emperor Tomb statues that is considered the Eighth Wonder of the World. It took 700,000 workers to complete 8000 life size statutes. From 200 BC to 200 AD the Han Dynasty ruled. Here Confucianism developed and expanded. Confucianism began about 500 BC. Hard to believe that is so long ago. A state was created with expanding economic powers and powerful centralization.

Confucian government pursuing legalist moral goals with an autocratic state became the normal political structure for the next 2000 years. To advance politically, one had to be a Confucian. That structure still exists today, the strong Communist Party with an expanding economy. This builds cohesion and power. During this time China was one of the wealthiest and innovative empires on earth.

The period from 600-900 AD is considered the Golden Age of Culture during the Tang Dynasty. The Ming Dynasty ruled from 1368-1644, when Tibet was absorbed into China. The last dynasty, Qing, lasted until 1911, when it collapsed and was replaced by the Republic of China led by Sun Yatsen, the first President and leader not an emperor. A tumultuous period followed until 1949 when the Republic collapsed during the great Chinese Civil War after World War II. During the later stage of the Qing Empire, about 1850 to 1911, China turned inward in response to foreign intrusion. Foreign trade was limited as outsiders long had been considered "barbarians" beneath Chinese civil standards. The ruling class believed China was the greatest empire and scorned outsiders. Foreign country ambassadors were requested to kneel before the ruling class, and their refusal angered the Qing government.

During the time from 1850-1911 China was invaded from Great Britain, France, and the United States with a policy known as "gunboat diplomacy". These countries under the guise of civilizing China, anchored warships in numerous Chinese ports, terrifying governments and the local populations to bend them to their will and enact unfair one-sided treaties. It was a form of imperialism allowing western countries to expand their empires inexpensively, without large occupying armies. The purpose was to intimidate technologically backward Asian countries. The stated excuse or rationale was to civilize these unknown and unfamiliar cultures that had been hostile to contact with outsiders for decades (sound a little familiar?). And of course, the trade commerce treaties increased the economic benefits for the Western powers. It also gave the western new naval iron steam riverboats an adventuresome mission. For instance, to see how extensively China was penetrated by foreigners, the British through force came to control the opium trade about 1845 and encourage its use. Opium was devastating China and was very lucrative. Two wars were fought from 1845-1875 in which China was defeated and humiliated which also meant they could not protect their citizens from the horrible effects of opium addiction. The British Navy blockaded and bombarded ports and were given many benefits at the Treaty of Nanking. British citizens were given immunity from Chinese courts and law enforcement and forced China to pay large reparations. More ports were opened to foreign trade with trade agreements favorable to Britain. Hong Kong was ceded to Britain, and in 1997 over 100 years later, it was returned to the People's Republic of China.

China continued to view foreigners as hostile and inferior. The West humiliated a former great empire, and that has not been forgotten to this day. From 1910-1940 US ships patrolled major China coastal rivers and ports. Today, 2019, gunboat diplomacy still continues as the US Naval 7th Fleet patrols the lengthy coast of China to "protect its Asian areas of influence". The Fleet is the largest forward-deployed

Fleet with 60-70 ships, 300 aircraft, and 42,000 Navy and Marine military personnel. China is rapidly building its own navy to protect its coastline and natural areas of influence along its coast and the South China Sea. It has 496 ships compared to the USA with 430, but many are older smaller or have less firepower and advanced electronics. But many Chinese smaller vessels have effective anti-ship cruise missiles. China is investing substantially in its Navy which is primarily defensive.

And let's not forget Japan invaded China in 1933 and occupied it until 1945 during WWII. Millions of Chinese civilians and soldiers lost their lives by another foreign invader.

In 2014 the Obama Administration shifted its military and diplomatic focus to China, calling this strategy the Pivot to China. How harmless it sounds. The US military now considers China a potential enemy and is reorganizing its forces to fight a major war in Asia. The Deep State pundits are accepting this policy. The US is trying to contain China and considers it a threat to US hegemony and worldwide economic dominance. Or we can call the US the leading nation, it's a nicer phrase. Sixty per cent (60%) of the USA air and naval combat assets with modern weapon platforms are now deployed in Asia from Japan and South Korea southward along the China coast to Malaysia, Vietnam, and the Philippines (1900 miles/3066 km). The US Fleet patrols the South China Sea which China considers its own. This concerns and upsets the Chinese government. The US and China have begun a long-term contest for influence in the area. America's democratic model is being tested by China and control over Asia is part of that strategy. Remember, China is an old venerable empire.

Where am I going with this discussion? Just like Russia, China is again becoming a proud powerful empire as it was for 20 centuries. So, what else would you expect than have China assert itself along its borders as areas of interest?

So, look again at the map of the Chinese military defense posture. Its coast line is protected by electronic anti-aircraft missiles and cruise attack missiles to defend itself against attacking navies (the USA Fleet). China is also building many more modern attack submarines to track enemy submarines and has sophisticated cruise missiles to attack surface ships. These missiles are called "carrier killers" that can sink or severely damage the US Fleet. They are the DF-21D and DF-21C missiles that have a range of 1800 km or 1000 miles. They have over 100 missiles with shorter ranges of 500km or 300 miles, the DF-15B.

China has also claimed a series of disputed islands in the South China Sea where the US Fleet has been patrolling upsetting China. Twenty-five per cent (25%) of the world's oil flows through here on tankers making this a very strategically important area for an empire. It is also an important military asset to maintain control of the South China Sea. Key strategic assets are the tiny Spratly and Parcel island chains. China intends to keep them regardless of what the US does militarily. Recently the US fleet sailed near them, an excellent way to antagonize China, and open old wounds. China is expanding its military presence over the South China Sea by building a military base on them to protect its traditional areas of influence and impress their foreign neighbors who also want a claim over the islands. This also translates into favorable regional economic influence and power. Remember the US excluded China from the now defunct Trans Pacific Partners Trade Agreement? What message that did that send to China?

The new military presence is considered appropriate national defense within China's area of influence and not offensive militarism. This is China's way of exerting influence over nearby smaller nations. This also raises the potential cost of any US intervention in the area. China has 60 naval ships and submarines in the area and a contingent of combat troops. It also is a potential attack force that could be used to control and isolate Taiwan from American naval influence. You can see how the US and China could be butting heads here, creating the setting for a military confrontation.

The US has about 14 large military bases in Japan, South Korea, Okinawa, Singapore, Philippines, Guam, and Australia. Three are very large naval bases in Guam, Singapore, and Japan. Military personnel (4000) are also stationed in Taiwan on their bases. These cover the length of the Chinese coast. Recently China sent its one aircraft carrier into the Taiwan Strait, (the sea between China and Taiwan), seemingly upset about a new US policy that creates closer political and cultural contacts between the US and Taiwan officials, as a show of power to Taiwan. That reminds them that China still considers Taiwan part of the People's Republic of China. And always will.

Nearby nations have nervous concerns about Chinese economic and military coercion. They want joint US exercises, ship visits, and intelligence sharing. The US is trying to hold China down, which could have serious unintended consequences.

So we have a situation like Russia as I said. China is becoming a cohesive nationalistic state and returning to its roots as a major Asian and worldwide power. Respected and not to be taken lightly. It also has been humiliated, attacked, and defeated by foreign powers and don't forget that also occurred fairly recently in 1931-45 by Japan.

Did I mention the Mongol occupation from 1225-1378 just like their Russian occupation?

CHINA HAS JUST BUILT A LARGE FOREIGN MILITARY BASE IN DJIBOUTI, AFRICA, ON THE HORN OF AFRICA near Somalia, Yemen, and Saudi Arabia, a very strategic location. The countries have good relations. Guess what? The USA has 4,600 troops stationed there and is not happy about it. China is also BUILDING 2 MORE large ports in Pakistan one of which it intends to use as a large naval and air force base. If Pakistan defaults on the commercial port loan, then China will take control of the port as collateral for the loan and operate and control it over a 99-year lease. Pakistan will also receive $50 BILLION OF CHINESE INFRASTRUCTURE AID for various important infrastructure projects. The countries have a close relationship. A port project built by China in Sri Lanka, the island nation next to India, also has had financial difficulties paying off a huge Chinese loan. China has recently taken control of this port under a new 99-year lease as payment for the defaulted loan and can make part of it a military base I believe. The original cost of the port in 2010 was $1.5 billion. China has made a large investment of $15 billion in Sri Lanka since 2005. This gives China a presence near important ocean shipping lanes and also is a port to provide access for its exports to India. And as a military base.

All this is part of China's One Belt One Road development strategy to provide funds for massive infrastructure projects in 68 countries that includes 4 billion people and 40% of world GDP. With this financial infrastructure connection countries are likely to cooperate with China on other military and diplomatic issues.

Countries highly indebted to China: Djbouti $100 billion; Kyrgystan $60 billion; Laos $40 billion; Mongolia $40 billion; Tajikstan $80 billion; Pakistan $15 billion but all debt is $80 billion (all are geographically important although very small in size)

CHINA IS also ALLIES WITH IRAN and buys 22% of Iran's oil exports. That is 6% of China's massive oil needs. Clearly a close relationship. China also invests in Iranian oil and gas infrastructure. So has Russia. In December 2018, Russia cancelled a $50 billion investment in oil and gas exploration in Iran primarily due to US economic sanctions. In August 2017 Russia and Iran signed a $2.5 billion deal to rebuild Iran's decaying rail system. It will reduce rail time between Mumbai, India and Moscow by 50%. It will increase Iranian trade and GDP, their economic well-being. All this has been made possible by lifting Iranian sanctions. All of this without any expensive military campaigns. And a win-win deal for all parties. The US cannot stop this investment anymore. It makes no sense for the US to unilaterally impose sanctions again as Iran has followed the rules regarding ceasing constructing nuclear capabilities as of August 2018. BAD idea USA. UPDATE: US has imposed more sanctions on Iran and any other country that does business with it. China and India are resisting these sanctions and have stated they will continue to buy Iranian oil but as a concession to the US reduce their consumption moderately. Russia will continue to trade with Iran but on a barter only basis. Canada and France cancelled plans for large Iranian investments. This is a dangerous situation. The US has presented no new data that Iran has violated any terms of the multi-country nuclear deal. I hate to say it, but it looks like the USA is acting as a provocative bully, AGAIN. I am not proud of this American policy. Like in Venezuela, the US is using economic sanctions extremely harmful to the average person of each country. As usual the biased US media mentions nothing about this consequence. Make the people suffer to bring these countries to their knees. Does anyone out there see this strategy as wrong? Morality? Huh?

So as I said the US has already lost a conventional military war or conflict against China. Did you notice the length of the Chinese coastline defended by defensive missiles? And the attack submarines? If for some unforeseen reason the US and China began a war it would be naval and air. The US Army and marines would not have the time to mass forces for a coastal or airborne invasion. China would know where they are (cannot hide in today's era of electronic and satellite warfare). Medium and

long-distance missiles and aircraft would begin to devastate these naval forces immediately. A US naval offshore bombardment with missiles and aircraft would be exposed to very heavy modern anti-aircraft fire and Chinese defensive land to sea counter missiles (including new carrier killer missiles). The US would inflict damage along the coastline to military positions and infrastructure with some urban civilian destruction scattered along the coastline. But the naval fleet would be exposed and easily detectable to Chinese weapons and in the flurry of furious firepower some would be hit, damaged, or sunk. This conflict would be over in about two weeks at most (or two days). The American people would never tolerate US Servicemen being killed and modern naval ships being sunk over another far away nebulous conflict that does not threaten America's homeland. Most likely this conflict would be about Taiwan. The US Fleet would turn around and head east out of range as the Navy could not tolerate seeing the Fleet heavily damaged and threatened with destruction. And guess what? The activated Chinese military without US presence would easily occupy Taiwan and claim it as a part of the People's Republic of China, and China would dominate Southeast Asia and achieve worldwide respect as the new empire and world leader. I don't think the US wants this. It should be very careful with its aggressive diplomacy and military strategy, and not antagonize and inadvertently fight China in their historical area of influence. The US should not be overconfident.

And don't forget, China will be using its economic strength to build and fund foreign infrastructure projects worldwide, winning friends and influencing countries. This could also be a subtle form of the new Chinese empire gaining territorial control in strategic assets. The Chinese also have plenty of time, they are in no hurry. They are convinced their power and economy will continue to grow. Just wait and watch.

And if nations default and cannot repay any Chinese loans, China will assume control of the project and the nation state will then pay rent to China. But China will maintain control over a strategic asset to their strategic advantage. Look, when I was a bank loan officer we did the same thing. In the event of default, we would take over a major project, and hire an outside contractor to manage it back to profitability, so we could recoup our major investment. That's how corporate project finance works.

Ok, here is my recommendation what the USA Defense Strategy should be. And I thought this up myself after writing this section, just me while I was driving my car to Starbucks for a Grande Latte and a Cheese Danish, warmed up. Driving, that's where some of my best ideas just pop up.

READERS NOTES:

SHOULD THE USA MILITARY PURSUE A LESS AGGRESIVE MILITARY INTERNATIONAL PRESENCE? WHY OR WHY NOT ?

USA CAPITOL

THE US MILITARY BUILD-UP AND CHINA (possibly not such a good idea)

A recent internet article by Lara Seligman in Foreign Policy, October 8, 2018, "US Puts Money Where Its Mouth is on China" illustrates the US military build up to counter a perceived Chinese East Asian threat to US influence and regional countries. Here is a list.

-15 F-35's

-Training armaments for infantry close combat

-More smart bomb guidance systems

-Modernize nuclear deterrent

-Fortify missile defense in Alaska, California, and Europe

-Upgrade Army Abrams tanks

-Expand naval fleet from 256 to 355 ships over 10 years

-Advanced new technology

　　　*Artificial intelligence systems

　　　*Hypersonic weapons that can travel at 5 times the speed of sound, 4000 miles per hour.

New US Pentagon policy considers China a major military threat and is preparing to fight a major land war against China if necessary.

MY PROPOSED USA 4 POINT POLICY PLAN:

 <u>Build up cyber defense</u>. Offensive can tag along. Protect all key military and corporate interests. Connect all military and intelligence services and key corporate industries to a massive anti-cyberwarfare interruption system. Public utilities, defense companies, communication and media, transportation, and high tech and social media companies would be protected by one system. Protect the USA from being shut down and vulnerable. This is a national coordinated effort, like the Internet was starting in 1985.

<u>Emphasize the buildup of a quick stealth attack submarine</u> fleet with advanced conventional weapons. China and Russia are continuing to do this, stealth like subs with advanced electronics and weapons. Attack subs do not usually deliver nuclear ballistic missiles. They find and harass surface ships and enemy submarines and do reconnaissance. The US has 71 submarines. Russia has 67, China has 63, some newly built to replace the noisy older ones. By 2020 China will have 69-78 submarines. According to Captain Jim Fannel, retired US Navy Director of Naval Intelligence of the Pacific Fleet, "make no mistake, China's long-term goal is to displace the US Navy as the largest and most capable submarine force in the world" (<u>The Economist</u> March, 2018). Many of these new ships will have China's new supersonic anti-ship cruise missile which the Pentagon considers lethal. All this is part of what China calls "non-contact warfare", the use of platforms and weapons capable of fighting long range precision attacks from outside an enemy's defended zone. See what I said about the US fleet being hit by missiles? Retreating. And never getting close to the Chinese mainland. (<u>The National Interest</u>). Attack submarines along coastlines can also fire to naval targets without being detected. Russia also uses submarines as escorts to their nuclear missile submarine fleet.

<u>Win the space race war. Whoever obtains the technology to disable enemy satellites first will dominate the world. The US Airforce has made this a top priority.</u>

On the TV show 60 Minutes, the new laser beam space ray was displayed which has been developed in New Mexico, not far from my home. It tracks and disables satellites. It is surreal and looks like a weapon from the old TV science fiction series <u>Flash Gordon.</u> Immense underground doors open up from the desert and two gigantic laser ray guns rise up to be aimed at outer earth space. Incredible. US Space Commander General John Raymond was on C-Span TV recently during a Congressional hearing and emphasized the Air Force space war weapon development program. I was impressed. To my mind this is the most important mission of the US Department of Defense. It makes sense. No human casualties. No infrastructure or cities destroyed. No radiation. You knock out another country's weapons, spy, and communication satellites and an entire country is rendered helpless and disabled. The idea is to get your technology there ahead of your opponent, so they cannot launch a significant counterattack against US satellites. You would not need to destroy all satellites. Just hit a few and intimidate the other side to bend to your will and neutralize all their space race technology and weapons. Checkmate it's over. The threat of being disabled by another country would force a country to submit to their will. And if your communications eyes and ears are gone, some madman leader could launch a nuclear attack and wipe out the other country, god forbid! So, now US, Russia, China, each of you must work tirelessly to win the space race war because there will be only one winner. If all three countries reach this level of technology close to one another and is afraid to use it, the we will again be in a position of Mutually Assured Space War Destruction just like the cold war, but permanently. Spies will be in demand, a new career path for college students.

Talk about action and espionage. Makes the TV show The Americans look like kids stuff! Holy Cow!! Yikes!!

So this brings us to #4. The only peaceful solution.

THE USA MUST develop very sophisticated highly educated foreign policy diplomats. A functioning State Department with a long-term goal of stabilizing the world, not primarily pursuing US ideological interests here and there all over the world. Not criticizing and pronouncing other countries enemies. China and Russia must perceive the US as not engaging them as a hostile competitor. The world is big enough to share (1984 anybody?). The US must treat these countries with respect and walk a fine line between any overt or covert military operations and plans towards them, while at the same time maintaining an effective military in the background to be used as needed. And all three countries must encourage each other's economic development and have positive reciprocal trade agreements that intertwine one another. A prosperous unthreatened country is a satisfied happy unaggressive country. And don't be concerned how each country is ranked in size of their economy. And realize each has longstanding important geo-political interests around their own borders based upon years of history that at least have to be understood and negotiated if there is a conflict. There must be compromise without fear. The USA, China, and Russia are not interested in conquering and managing each other's countries, are they? This isn't fascist WWII. Why is the USA so fearful all the time? Three large nations fearful and distrustful of one another will eventually engage in a harmful war of some kind. We are all lucky no nukes were fired during the Cold War, a period of 47 years. Don't count on that again.

In a recent speech I viewed on CSPAN by Xi Jinping, the President of China, at the economic conference at Hainan Province, he said keenly that the Cold War and the era of the zero-sum game is over. It is the time for win-win solutions and worldwide cooperation, treating other countries as equals and with respect. Having State to State political and economic partnerships, restraining from dominance, rejecting hegemony, and safeguarding peace while supporting education, health, and youth. Excellent. Bravo.

And like in my earlier section THE SURGE, real strength is a strong expanding economy with opportunity for its people. Not the number of nuclear weapons.

The United States is draining its resources to support an unnecessary military and foreign policy paradigm (ideological strategy) that is causing suffering around the world due to the unintended consequences of having an aggressive pro-active interventionist policy to protect life and liberty. The USA has been at war continually from 1990 until today, 2018, with no end in sight. There is something wrong about this picture.

The USA is making enemies one step at a time. Credibility is ebbing.

GEORGE KENNAN, a great American Diplomat and foreign policy expert in the 1940's and 1950s' was Ambassador to Russia. He devised the Containment Theory to keep the Soviet Union from expanding and spreading communist ideology. But he emphasized economic and political containment, not a gigantic military encirclement. What I write now below is based on his ideas and public statements and writing. He was a foreign policy realist. So was Henry Kissinger and President Richard Nixon. Every elected President since Nixon has been an idealist which is to a large extent the root cause of the failure of the USA foreign policy and military action. What do I mean?

From the time of the American Founding Fathers in 1787 to Woodrow Wilson in 1917 the US emphasized Balance of Power diplomacy and did not espouse US involvement and criticism of another country's political policies and ideology. This idea goes all the way back to 1648 and the Treaty of Westphalia in Europe. It emphasized state sovereignty and the right of each state to determine its own policies without outside interference. All States must respect the legal entity of another state. All states are equal and must live in peace with all other states. No one State shall have an overwhelming advantage to war and intimidate other states. This shall be offset by treaties and alliances of various states that prevent this from occurring. Thus, states with different ideologies could form alliances to insure peace.

This was a consequence of the very bloody 30 years' war in Central Europe, fought over religious doctrine, Catholics fighting Protestants.

Wilsonian idealism since 1918 has influenced US foreign policy until today with its emphasis on morality as statecraft emphasizing the spread of democracy and morality (the US and western European viewpoint) into other countries. And dominance and control over weaker states (Latin America from 1960-1990). In 1972 President Nixon and Secretary of State Henry Kissinger negotiated the SALT Treaty (Strategic Arms Limitation Treaty) limiting nuclear weapons production and usage with Russia/Soviet Union and went to China to open a relationship to foster peace and understanding which was non-existent for decades. Both countries were directly opposed to US ideology and considered enemies. These US initiated overtures were not idealism but were to reduce tensions and the possibility of war. Practical, realistic, not ideological, that was set aside.

I am going to list a selection of Kenan's ideas and comments. after WWII.

"At the bottom of the Kremlin' neurotic view of world affairs is the traditional and instinctive sense of insecurity and fear of the outside world."

"...(Kenan) urge the US government to withdraw from its public advocacy of democracy and human rights...(and) the tendency to see ourselves as the center of political enlightenment and as teachers to a great part of the rest of the world strike me (Kenan) as unthoughtful, vainglorious, and undesirable".

In 1996 he opposed the war in Kosovo and expansion of NATO. He said these policies would hurt relations with Russia. It has indeed.

"The best thing we can do if we want the Russians to let us be Americans, is to let the Russians be Russian". I have said that in this book.

It is pertinent today. A rebirth of an empire and fear of the West. Enough said.

NOTE: JUST saw this on C-Span TV, May 26, 2018. Here they are, the DEEP STATE viewpoint!! This is a panel discussion sponsored by the Center for National Interest, a Washington think tank analyzing key foreign issues. From what I saw they present a USA/Eurocentric condescending attitude towards Russia as weak and inferior, implying the current Russian State as illegitimate and not-sustainable. There was much discussion about how to subdue Russian challenges. There seemed to be a general consensus including the audience that Russia had to be carefully controlled. Could they be implying the magic words REGIME CHANGE? This is an excellent example of the "Deep State Vapor "(or Deep State Attitude). Not an organized formalized underground movement, but ideas that swirl around, are reinforced by discussions, captivate people's viewpoints, spread like a contagion, impose unanimity, conformity. Remember the popular classic 1956 movie. "The Invasion of the Body Snatchers?" The alien people impersonators put organic pods next to people's beds at night which opened and absorbed them, made them controlled zombie-like automatons. Well? What do you think? Panelists: I am putting them in so you can see their background. The former CIA Deputy Director Intelligence for Eurasia; the former Under Secretary Senior Advisor to President George W. Bush; the former CIA Officer and Station Chief 1964-94, the former CIA Russian Analysis Chief, Special Advisor to Vice President D. Cheney, Center for National Interest Intelligence and National Security Director. He seemed to be a realist in that he stated that the USA and Russia do not have an insurmountable ideological difference today as during the Cold war but have interests and behaviors that conflict but that could be fixed. This leaves hope for a peaceful future.

Former United States Secretary of Defense Honorable James Mattis

Here is a list of countries that the US has directly or covertly encouraged Regime Change since 2011 or that is also on the radar screen for increased future Regime Change. This can also include seriously weakening current governments enhancing US regional and world influence.

North Korea, Cuba, Venezuela, Libya, Tunisia, Egypt, Yemen, Iran, Iraq, Syria, Palestine, Kyrgyzstan, Georgia, Ukraine, Afghanistan, Russia (the Big Prize).

And here's another list of some of the international leaders the US fought or eliminated that initially represented the fight for their people's national independence and freedom from oppression (but sometimes they became oppressive).

Bad Guys for the US, Good Guys for Others

Ho Chi Minh-Vietnam   2. Patrice Lumumba-Congo   3. Fidel Castro & Che Guevara-Cuba   4. Salvador Allende-Chile   5. Mao Tse Tung-China   6. Vladimir Lenin-Russia   7. Mohammad Mosaddegh-Iran

8. Fred Hampton-Black Panthers   9. Russell Means, Dennis Banks, Leonard Peltier (in prison over 40 years and ill health)-American Indian Movement   10. Hugo Chavez-Venezuela

All have passed away except Leonard Peltier who is in prison 40 years so far.

US Special Forces Reconnaissance patrol Afghanistan

AFGHANISTAN---Still going on after 18 years. Time flies when you're having fun. [American expression] The long-term siege of this country reminds me of the lengthy border war against the Germanic and Celtic tribes by the Roman Empire beginning about 100 AD for over 200 years which was a bloody expensive stalemate. It helped bankrupt the Roman Empire. Rome could never subdue these tribes defending their homeland. Eventually these tribes invaded and sacked Rome. Destroyed it.

Something is wrong with this strategy. This is part of the new militarization of American political thought. To get out of this ungodly mess and save as many innocent Afghans and US troops as possible I recommend the following: All troops leave the country except about 10,000 currently there now to create two large garrisons around the capitol city Kabul and Kandahar in the south. Special Forces units would probe the perimeters to provide reconnaissance and combat missions to keep the surrounding forces off balance. US and NATO F-16's and Drones would provide air support. All citizens who desire to emigrate would be provided a substantial stipend for relocation expenses to designated countries and 5 years of living expenses. The Taliban and rural Warlords (huge heroin producers) would then have time to consolidate the country (a few years) and then the US could evacuate the country and let Afghanistan govern itself. The current situation is endless.

I do not understand this American paranoia or fear of being overcome by worldwide enemies.

The USA does not have to win everything and dominate. This fear and national anxiety cause over reactions to occur such as military and economic aggression and a false sense of glory and self-importance. And as far as spreading the word of liberal democracy fervently around the world as the answer to every country's destiny, remember the original USA Founding Fathers were wealthy white men who did not trust the mass of citizens, but were concerned they could be easily influenced by radical leaders with extreme ideology. That is why the Senate was elected by the House of representatives until the 17th Amendment was passed in 1913. The country was run by an elite to protect its own property interests and was not entirely democratic. Think of George Washington, Thomas Jefferson, Benjamin Franklin, John Adams, Alexander Hamilton, and John Hancock.

Amidst all this conflict I sometimes think the American Indians had it right. The Plains Indians spiritual ceremony, the Sweat Lodge, should be required of all national leaders and important people. They need to get connected and centered with their inner soul and sense of self. Participation is a transformative experience. The intense heat, darkness, glowing red-hot stones, melodic singing and chanting, and drumming goes deep inside you. All this intensity causes momentary stress and fear which clears away your daily reality and thoughts, opening yourself up to new realities and clarity. After all the USA or America, is the Native Americans land or ground. I have been in this ceremony many times and it is transformative, challenging, and inspiring.

GUN *VIOLENCE IN THE USA and elsewhere-a short commentary*

This has to stop. I am viewing the massive demonstrations across the USA on March 24, 2018 by the young people and also those not so young. It is very moving and makes sense. Millions of people in major cities. ASSAULT WEAPONS MUST BE BANNED AND OTHER GUN RULES PUT INTO PLACE TO MANAGE THIS PROBLEM. This is not the Wild West in 1875. Have you ever fired an assault weapon? I have in US Army Basic Training. The M16 assault rifle and the AR 15 are about the same. Extremely terrifying and deadly. Made to kill and maim. That was at Fort Ord California in 1971. It is made of dark

black metal and hard plastic.

When you fire it from the standard military prone position the butt is up against your chin. It vibrates and brangs and sends vibrations into you as each round is fired, accurately at targets 300-400 yards away. I always felt as if I had this lethal cobra in my hands and arms. We were always told it is our best friend as it could save your life. Fired on fully automatic it discharges 36 rounds and could literally cut you in half. The round tumbles so it tears your flesh and organs apart as it goes through you. It can hit your arm and spin through you and exit from your back. A beautifully designed weapon to kill humans. I teach in a college and high school. The day either teachers or students are allowed to carry guns is the day I never step on a campus again. Teachers can also do crazy violent acts or fire a weapon accidentally while examining it. It would be terrifying to have a militarized faculty. And college students. I would be terrified someone would get a poor grade and shoot me. All A's in my classes for sure.

All this is part of the militarization of America after 27 years of war since 1990. (Thanks, Neo-Cons). Political leaders and other important people do not support assault weapons unless you have fired one. And the National Rifle Association and Congress shame on you.

I respect the police but the police have engaged in wanton purposeful killings-we have all seen it.

This provides a terrible example to would be killers. And it's not only the officers, but the training officers, police chiefs and mayors that should be held accountable. The USA is providing a terrible image to the world. It could be so much better; the USA would be a shining example to the world. It would make a statement which denounces violence in our society, providing a new less violent culture. How can we preach freedom and peace to the world, just ask me that.

And foreign enemies? Is there gun violence in China, Russia, and Iran? And Poland, Sweden, Germany, France, Great Britain, Japan, South Korea, and Canada?

As of June 2018, there were 154 mass shootings involving 4 or more people in the USA. 11,000 people are killed by firearms each year.

And Black Lives DO Matter. How many unarmed blacks have been gunned down in cold blood by white police officers? Do police in England gun down perpetrators? How many white men have been gunned down by police?

It's all part of a culture of violence. It is incredibly easy to get a firearm. Europe would be shocked if they understood this. The military sends assault equipment to cities. Vets come back from war combat hardened and perhaps internally stressed. I had a student who had been in Iraq seven years ago who had serious PTSD and was still under treatment. He told me he needed a calm classroom and shouldn't sit near anyone and I shouldn't talk about any anti-US Army-Iraq issues. He said if he was agitated he would exit the room. He was OK. We sent him to counseling. He got a B. I felt sorry an unneeded corrupt war had harmed him. He is a victim.

Another time 7 years ago at Noon I was in a crowded McDonalds parking lot. I was sitting in my car eating lunch. In front of me was a car with several army ranger stickers (that's ok). Three 12-year-old girls went out of the car to get hamburgers. And standing by the car door was a man, probably their father, with a pistol in a holster on his hip. It intimidated me. I was nervous. I was going to object, but he stared at me, so I broke off eye contact and went back to my lunch. I will never forget that. Open carry is legal in New Mexico. So let's not forget. I am now 72 and opposed to assault weapons and gun intimidation unequivocally. It is not just the child mass shootings. It affects everybody. People are proud of saying the US is a peace loving Christian nation. 305 million guns in the USA, an armed nation, is not what the New Testament professes, not what Jesus taught. Easy access to assault weapons and guns is just irresponsible. That's it.

In 1999 while driving across the Pine Ridge Indian Reservation I picked up a hitchhiker, a 28 year old Lakota who was a US Army sniper during the first Iraq War Desert Storm. Nine years had passed. He said he shot and killed 106 Iraqi soldiers. He kept count!

Some victims just dropped when hit and others twitched until stopping. He was in extreme anguish and guilt suffering terrifying dreams and anxiety all day.

He was beginning to see a Medicine spiritual man to try and heal during spiritual Lakota ceremonies. A real shame. A casualty of war. There are many many others. Including those in countries the US attacked.

IMMIGRATION-A few observations

On immigration, well, I live in New Mexico. And I don't know who is an illegal and who isn't. But we have had a lot of immigration. Forty-seven percent of the state is Hispanic. Forty percent Caucasian. Twelve percent American Indian, Native American. And one percent other, being Asian and African American. Actually, in the last seven years, immigration has stopped more or less. It's actually reversing itself. There's a little more flow back to Mexico as that economy has improved. Now I don't know if the illegals are the same way, but it probably is similar. And illegals do a lot of wonderful things in this country and support the economy. If there were no so-called illegals doing all of the gardening in the middle-class and upper-class suburbs and working on golf courses, there'd be a huge shortage of labor for those jobs. And I could probably get a $30 an hour summer job cutting grass! Green fees for golfers would rise. All this would really hit the budgets hard for middle-class people, who use all these people to get inexpensive gardening, grass mowing, fixing their flowers, doing odd jobs. Illegals also do a lot of work that is really undesirable, like working in packing plants where they kill chickens and cattle and gut them, and work in that really harsh environment and do a lot of the tough work. And they work on large corporate California farms. These farm owners are very concerned because migrant workers are leaving the workforce to return to Latin America for fear of being arrested and jailed causing labor shortages which will lead to higher food and wine prices or shortages. Heaven forbid! What will we do with a shortage of your favorite California wine. They do a lot of the picking of vegetables and grapes in California. And I know there's nannies. Many are older women who take care of small children. Many are in Chicago, my home town. And they're from countries like Belize and Honduras. They're great Americans (just not citizens yet). They work for cash. They actually do pretty well, and are responsible. They have apartments. And they become a part of their families who employ them. It's a win-win. They help our American society. I know one. These "immigrants" also send huge amounts of money back to Mexico to help their families. After oil exports this is the largest source of foreign money. America gets low wage workers for rough jobs and Mexico gets financial help. A good trade.

I have no opinion here about the Trump Wall and the current border amnesty immigration. It needs a humane solution without fear.

Washington Monument

Is the US leaving up to the ideals of the Founding Fathers?

THE UNITED STATES ECONOMY-BIG

Another topic I just want to discuss is the economy, the US economy, the world economy,

and I have talked about it in this book. I'm an economics instructor, professor, and I know something of what I'm talking about in terms of general economic trends. I'm not going to talk about it all.

But one thing we have to think about regardless of our philosophy and our leaders' philosophy towards economics, politically and socially, is we need a plan, a bipartisan plan to create an economy that has long-term sustainability -- and I use that word "sustainability"-- of economic growth with fairness and opportunity. This economy shouldn't be going up and down like a yo-yo based on quick changing expedient policies about interest rate targets and government spending and taxation. And when I say sustainable it doesn't just mean growth, it means good growth. Growth in national defense, in healthcare for sickness, for police is not good growth because those are social problems that need to be fixed by society that cost money that needs to be used for other priorities. But these institutions do need funding to solve these problems for fixing negative things: crime, disease, war, that we need less of. We need growth to build the society, human capital, physical capital, infrastructure, financial support for the needy, for seniors, education, parks and more. We need sustainable growth, and an economy that is providing good jobs for people that pay to sustain a middle class, which is most of the country frankly. It's like 70 percent of the country. And then add the people near the bottom who need help as well (50 million below the poverty level of $12,000 per person). And 80 million total people under $25,000. One-half of the US population has no-that's ZERO-- net worth. Really. Check it out. I'm one of them now. It is tough and comes with much anxiety. Do you know that the largest group in poverty is single women with children at 28% of the total number in poverty and that 50% of children are born into single parent households in the USA? A new normal. Under the Trump paid maternity leave proposal only married women would receive assistance. Is that really moral, compassionate, in light of these statistics?

Also let me remind you that 26 Blue States, Republican controlled, rejected the Medicaid expansion to include people at $18,000 yearly income, or 150% of the poverty level. Just to let you know, 48 million people in the USA are on food assistance, or SNAP. This is up from 22 million prior to the 2009 recession. And the federal budget for this has doubled from $44 billion to $88 billion today. Interesting that this number did not decline during the steady go-slow economic expansion of the past 8 years. Why?

Because many of the new jobs are at very low salaries and many people are discouraged and dropping out of the labor force into the underground cash economy. And the benefit is small and typically ranges from $50 to $250 per month. Try eating on that. It also cannot be used to buy non-food items like tooth paste, tissue paper, and Tylenol. I would double the budget but then at $180 billion it would be 30% of the US Defense Budget! And providing people with enough food is not going to cause them to work less. I disagree with the argument that support makes people lazy and satisfied being poor with some subsistence benefits.

Income Distribution—Class Warfare Reversed

One of the biggest problems we have is income distribution. There's too much economic power at the top, and that translates into political power. It's a fact of life, the top one percent, 10 percent, have got most of the income and wealth growth in the last 30, 40 years. Since 2010, 95% of all personal income growth has gone to the top 1%. Since 1975-80, the real income (that's income net of inflation) of the top one percent has grown at least 200%-300% percent plus the positive substantial wealth effect of stocks and other physical assets like real estate going up. The <u>USA has 46,250 people with a net worth in excess of fifty million dollars.</u> That is $50 million. The Dow Jones Industrial Average has increased from 6750 to 26200 since 2009, about a 2600% increase. Since 1980 the Dow Jones Average has increased from 1000 to 26000. Net of 2%-3% yearly inflation this is equivalent to 7500 or 750%. (a compounded rate of return of 9%, then add 2% dividends =11% per year). During this time real wage growth net of inflation for the bottom 70% is only up about 18% for the entire time period (37 years) NOT per year. For the bottom 50% there has been no wage growth after deducting inflation-virtually NO INCREASE in the standard of living. There's something wrong with this picture. In productivity, which has grown about two to three percent historically, wages haven't kept up with productivity. From 1945-75, as productivity increased two to three percent per year so did real wages, that is your increased wage net of the inflation. In 1975 inflation was about 13% and I received an 18% salary increase, or 5% in real terms, much better than today's raises. So that correlation diverged or split about 35 years ago, and that correlation of productivity to real wage growth is what built this country. I talk about it earlier in this book. Paul Krugman, a Nobel Prize winning economist, calls this era "The Grand Bargain" (1950-1975). As Government, Big Business, and Labor Unions grew, these groups cooperated with each other to build a strong flourishing economy. That was the period when the unions, the large growing US government, and the growing international corporate business communities all worked together with an unofficial understanding that they all needed one another to grow an economy to become a strong, successful country. And everybody got a piece of the pie. There wasn't as much cutthroat competition, but MORE COOPERATION, or a shared vision, AS THE US GREW INTO A STRONG WORLD LEADERSHIP POSITION. One example is that working as a corporate loan officer in a large bank was more like working for the government. It was difficult to get fired and lifelong employment and progress was the norm. Mediocre performers were just put into less rigorous positions. By 1975 that was changing into an intensely competitive performance environment with minimal job security, pressure, and constant change. No fun.

Of course the unions did their strikes, and that was just the way they got things done. Unfortunately, some companies got hurt. The sense of the public good seems to have been diminished these days. It was much more apparent in the '50s and '60s. Were people less conflicted, happier? I recommend that union leaders and representatives of the workforce be placed on corporate boards. Also, a US government observer reporting to the Department of Justice to insure corporate policies abide by the law. The elite, the top 1% of wealth, are very talented, and extremely highly compensated, and the rest of most of us have mediocre wage increases perhaps at best. So we need to keep that in mind. And when people talk about class warfare of the average person or the Democratic Party trying to take money through taxes from the wealthy, well, class warfare already occurred. The top took it from the middle and the bottom since 1980. We're just trying to readjust it. And I say we because I'm part of that idea. And I don't believe in soaking wealthy people or corporations with very high taxes, but perhaps they have to reconsider their fair share, especially since marginal tax rates were 50% to 90% for upper incomes when this country grew after World War II to just after Vietnam. (This is called the Golden Era). And now they're half that amount or less, 35%-40%. Capital gains taxes have been cut in half from 35% to 20%. The wealthy receive much of their income through dividends and sale of stocks and real estate. And capital gains have no Fica/Medicare tax of 7.45% or 14.9%. There is a 3.9% tax surcharge on capital gains for high incomes to help pay for Medicaid. That makes this tax 23.9%. The formula calculation makes it a little less. During the period prior to 2000 this total capital gains rate was about 35%. The current proposed US health care plan has eliminated this Medicaid tax (socialist public benefit surcharge-that's what it is, get used to the idea) causing a huge revenue shortfall for Medicaid and a reduction in health benefits for many people if enacted.

This tax is a form of socialism income redistribution. Is this bad? I ask you to think about it.

I just think we have to realize that to have income continually go to the top 10--15%, the economy is just not sustainable. That's why raising the minimum wage would help. It would take money away from stockholders and corporations and give it to their employees. Some companies, like Aetna, have raised the minimum wage to $16. So has Morgan Chase Bank. Jamie Diamond, their President, talked about this. Their minimum is $15 an hour plus good benefits. Amazon raised its minimum wage to $15.Theses corporations see the value of paying people well, which provides loyalty, more productivity and more efficiency for the company, and therefore better results. This helps all these employees. And yes, taking money away from stockholders is a form of socialism. So what about social security and food stamps-banish them? And employee rights? Are there any?

Isn't it morally correct and part of increasing the Public Good of our country, the USA, to keep income and wealth distribution from becoming too extreme? Some of us believe we should be running solo, totally independent and mostly responsible to only ourselves (including family). Others, like me, look at countries more as a cooperative beehive. We work together and share the abundance as needed but not stifling incentives to earn. The personal income minimum for the top 1% is $440,000 per year, for the top .1% it is $1,900,000, and 26,250 people in the US have a net worth greater than $50,000,000 as I have stated.

Corporations have to consider the Stakeholders, as they did after the post WWII growth period, not primarily just the stockholders as they do now, where it's all about earnings per share and higher stock prices. Who are these stakeholders? You and me. Employees, unions, retirees, communities, all branches of government. And remember a phrase "The Public Good"? Meaning following reasonable regulations, helping create policies that help many people, not just corporate interests.

REMEMBER: THE VAST MAJORITY OF THE POPULATION NEEDS GOOD INCOME TO BUY ALL THE PRODUCTS AND SERVICES PRODUCED BY CORPORATIONS AND THE ELITES [THE TOP 10%] TO MAKE THIS ECONOMY HUM, SO EVERYONE BENEFITS.

Get It??

Today, special powerful corporate business interests influence government policies to their advantage, as does very wealthy private money (Lobbying). Economists call this Rents (no value added to GDP). And many legislators and staff go to work for lobbying firms in the industry they tried to regulate at very high salaries, something they keep in mind. These corporations write much of the legislation that will affect them. Again, something is wrong with this picture. Congress now spends ½ of their time raising campaign money for their next election! Yes, indeed. US banks lobbied very hard in 1999-2000 to relax regulations to allow banks to engage in riskier trading of derivatives and other financial businesses. The Glass-Steagall Act was removed which prohibited banks from taking undue risks. My high school friend, a Senior Vice President, was instrumental in negotiating Citicorp's purchase of Traveler's Insurance which began this deregulation process. Citicorp was the largest US Bank and Travelers a huge insurance company. So what about the Public Good as a guideline for economic behavior, an attitude that says we are all in this together? After the 2008-09 financial collapse Congress enacted the Dodd-Frank Wall Street Reform and Consumer Protection Act which reduced bank risk taking and prevented financial abuses of consumers and homeowners. Now bank lobbyists are trying to lessen its impact. Back and forth, it never ends. The banks have actually benefited and are very profitable currently and have reduced their risk profile. But the largest 5 banks now own 50% of all US bank assets, up from 40% 10 years ago. In my day in the 1980's that number was about 6-8%. They are Morgan Chase, Wells Fargo, Bank of America, Goldman Sachs (really a premier investment banker) and Citicorp. All have seen a significant increase in their stock price except Citicorp. Their influence on the USA has also substantially increased.

JP MORGAN-CHASE BANK biggest in USA

MIXED ECONOMIES-----"ISMS"

I tell my students all the economies of the world are a blend of the public government sector and the private business free enterprise sector. We tend to refer to extensive government as socialism and the private sector as capitalism. I prefer a spectrum of a mixture between both sectors. The entire world economies are a blend of socialism and capitalism. This blend is based upon a country's history, culture, geography, resources, and political traditions. All are equally valid and should be respected and tolerated, none really better than the other. The degree of government involvement is based upon the percentage of money that flows through government, regulation, and economic planning. For instance, since 1800 the USA has been moving towards more government involvement as the complexity and need for government has increased. It's a new modern advanced world. I consider the US close to an even split of government and private enterprise. Total government spending, federal, state, local, ($7 trillion) is about 35% of US GDP ($20 trillion). The $7 trillion includes transfer payments like Social Security, Medicare/Medicaid, Food Stamps (SNAP), moderate housing assistance. The federal budget is $4.5 trillion, of which 50% is transfer payments. Total governmental spending at all levels excluding transfer payments is about 20% of GDP. The US also has many government regulations that increases government power.

So the US is partially socialist, like all countries. Western Europe has a much larger public government sector and is more socialist. Germany's public sector is 48% of GDP, Sweden 54% and France is 56% which also has the most regulation and individual benefits. Canada is 42%, Venezuela has moved from far-Right Wing or little public sector to substantial socialist public sector and benefits since the Bolivarian Revolution starting in 1998. In the past Venezuela had the highest level of income at the top and the highest poverty rate in South America. It declined substantially since introducing socialism but has been climbing since too much rapid change and poor economic planning has caused a terribly complicated and difficult economy and political situation. Due to food shortages the average person has lost weight. Russia and China have come from extreme socialism or communism (never really achieved as Karl Marx envisioned). They are heading towards free market economies with state supervision or management. Both understand free market economies provide prosperity and economic and political strength.

Their public benefits have declined over the past 25 years as the powerful state has diminished. They spend about 30%-40% on government. So you see every country is a blend and always in the process of change. Putin calls Russia "managed democracy" with a powerful state. China calls their economy "Socialism with Chinese Characteristics". Now the USA is in a titanic struggle between more government domestic spending and those who want to roll it back to give the private sector more room to grow. But we need both. Too little government engenders inequity and economic distress, hardships for society. Too much suffocates economic growth. I view capitalism and free markets as essential but in need of guidance, restraint, careful planning. Think of a giant pounding down Park Avenue in New York City, like a Godzilla movie, lurching side to side, crashing into buildings, smashing cars, people running and hiding, blowing fire from its mouth. Scary and unpredictable, lots of bad side effects, while it crashes down the street towards Central Park, its destination of a prosperous future. Now I see it restrained by many people holding it in place with ropes and barricades, gradually moving it slowly but steadily and safely to the Central Park, the promised land of prosperity. No negative side effects. But plenty of regulation and control. Safe. People unhurt. But just enough slack in the ropes to avoid dangerous spillover effects but still enough movement to economic prosperity. Companies that pollute are making more money for stockholders, by not spending on pollution control equipment. This lowers their manufacturing costs and increases profits. The society suffers a great cost and harm of health and the environment or must pay for cleanup with higher public taxes. Laws and fines make the polluter pay for its damage. When President Trump loosened coal mining regulations it boosted coal company's profits and some minor employment, but it will cause great economic harm to the environment and pollute streams and local communities drinking water. Mountain top surface mining in Appalachia has destroyed over 50 hilly mountains and caused widespread environmental damage.

People are sick from drinking contaminated ground water. The natural spirit of the forest and land is gone forever.

So, too little financial regulation and consumers suffer and risks to the economy increase. The 2008-09 economic crisis was caused by too little regulation of the financial system. Mortgage lending standards became irresponsible. In the 1960's the highly polluted Cleveland River caught on fire from chemicals from unregulated industrial waste. This has since been cleaned up and the river actually has fish. I drove through Smoky Mountain National Park. At high levels the trees are dying from air pollution from coal power plants 200 miles west, the Tennessee Valley Authority government project from the 1930's. Rain water pours into streams with evaporated chemicals and kills off fish and poisons the streams. True! These economic spill-over effects can kill a country.

To build a strong country you need a productive happy, healthy, well-paid workforce, new technological innovation, good education, safety and political stability, and a solid physical infrastructure. This is the background for any society that is necessary for the private economy to flourish and encourage entrepreneurs to innovate and take risks to create new good jobs. This is what the USA did between 1946 and 1975 and now this has been declining. Spending massive amounts of money on infrastructure and education is what has caused India and China to achieve high economic growth. The American Society of Civil engineers recently gave the United States a D+ grade on infrastructure, just pitiful for such an extraordinary country. This is slowing down the economy. The USA is really backsliding here.

As I have stated I recommend the Corporate Board of Directors be required by Federal law to create a democratic Board that represents stakeholders, not just stockholders. This would include representatives of labor unions, non-union workers, lower level management, and perhaps a non-voting representative of the US government reporting to the Federal Reserve Bank, a quasi-independent institution that regulates the economy. The Federal Reserve is free from the political influences that control US Agencies. This would apply to perhaps a few of the biggest corporate strategic industries (banks/financial, media, defense, health insurance, drugs, oil/energy, auto and heavy polluters).

Corporations might grant the government a tiny stockholder investment of .10%, which would hardly dilute current shareholders equity holdings. This would help "tame" capitalism and minimize harmful policies. These corporate reports would only be distributed and read by the President and the four key leaders in Congress, representative of the major political parties. Perhaps this is unrealistic.

More Wealth and Income Issues-The New Unemployment

So when you have severe distribution of wealth and income inequality eventually you have political instability and resentment, dissatisfaction. And that's occurring here in the United States. The top 1% have 40% of total US individual wealth up from 26% in 1975. And the bottom 80% have only 8% of the wealth. The average income of the top 1% of households is $440,000 compared to $58,000 for the rest of the population. The population considered middle class has dropped from 61% to 48% since 1971. based on their income. And there's no reason for this trend to stop unless there's fundamental changes made. The elite, the upper .01% of the adult population of 250 million, is very fortunate and may have worked very hard and possess extraordinary skills, talent, and intelligence, and luck. But in 1980 the bottom 90% had 65% of national income which declined to 50% in 2015. The median net worth per household is $80,000. Much wealth is home equity for the lower 65%. The vast majority of the population needs good income to purchase all the goods and services (all that stuff) provided by the top 1% to keep the economy robust. So we all benefit together, all of us, the economy, and are all INTERCONNECTED.

Trump voters consider this issue. You actually may benefit from some good old-fashioned income redistribution polices, like a higher minimum wage, higher marginal tax rates for the wealthy, and subsidized governmental benefits (like cheaper better health care, housing, education, food nutrition, roads, sewers, trains, airports, internet, parks, paid maternity leave and child care). And yes, all of this could be called "socialism". And all this good spending helps the economy and provide jobs too. And income taxes to pay for all of this. Better income with taxes due then no income and no taxes. My income of $33,000 means I am at the 69% level, or I earn more money than 31% of the population. When I was in banking 25 years ago I was in the top 12% compared to the bottom 31% now. I spend less and charge credit cards more.

As part of my little lesson here, I want to talk about unemployment and employment. We've had a big unemployment problem. And if you watch the news today, they talk about how low the unemployment rate has dropped, from 10.6% to 3.4% since 2009, and many new jobs have been created. But the problem is that many of them are not good jobs in terms of income. Many are part-time jobs and part-time workers. The USA considers part-time workers as employed in calculating the 3.4% rate. Or many are contract workers on short-term, multi-month contracts who are considered employed. And they could have very insecure employment and moderate pay, and low benefits, no medical. Many of these new jobs are in the retail and hospitality sectors that pay low. So it takes the oomph out of the economy, out of economic growth. It's not good for anybody. And this is what we have to look at. Plus a lot of the jobs have not been good paying jobs to the young college graduates. Many low paying jobs go to seniors, who are now starting to work part time, like myself, because we have to. I'm a part-time teacher, making $14,000 a year, plus $20,000 from Social Security. And in New Mexico, I get along with that, barely. Many professors live in a state of financial insecurity and uncertain employment through no fault of their own. So we have to be aware of this. In the past, unions were very strong in this country, and sure there was labor unrest but they struggled for rights, for workers' rights, better working conditions, benefits and salary. That's been diminished, taken apart, as our jobs have left and corporations and the laws and legal decisions made in this country have diminished the strength of unions. And you see it today in political campaigns. But unions built the country because once 33 percent of all workers in this country were in unions, let's say, in 1960-65. Now it is down to 9%, mostly public employee unions that are under attack from the Right Wing and The Freedom Party. They have an extreme free market ideology that strongly opposes government and are trying to reduce it or take it apart (except Defense and National Security). So when those unions got a big pay raise, it also spreads to the non-union companies, who had to keep pace to be competitive and pay their workers and also to stop unrest. So it raised wages for everybody. It wasn't as if the unions only benefited and the people not in the unions were not hired because there was a strong labor market. That's what people don't talk about. So I'm a teacher. Thank goodness I'm in a union. We've got some better benefits. We got a two percent raise rather than zero. And we have struggled to get better working conditions and resolved communication issues that make life better for everybody in our college. Globalization, which you may have heard about, which is the trend for industry and jobs to be located all over the world, that's going to continue. We can't just stop a long-term trend. The world is much more competitive with other nations opening up their economies. They are putting substantial funds into education and infrastructure to create new investment and long term employment opportunities. India and China are two good examples with GDP growth rates of 7-10%, versus 2% in the USA. Since about 1999 the US has lost 2,750,000 high paying manufacturing jobs to China. So what we need is retraining of the workforce where it's needed with substantial funds to pay for BOTH the education and a living allowance while people stop working to get educated. This also includes professional work related to this that requires retraining. But these are things are being ignored and overlooked. It is common knowledge that 3 million to 6 million highly skilled good paying jobs are unfilled due to lack of proper training and skills. And as I stated The American Society of Civil Engineers gave the USA a D+ grade on Infrastructure. The USA needs more and new infrastructure to build a thriving economy and create good jobs like China and India and some European countries. Germany has neglected infrastructure which is hampering their economy because they demand a too conservative balanced budget. The USA is really neglecting this important economic factor. It cannot continue this way. Ben Bernanke, former Federal Reserve Chairman, wrote recently that one of the most important factors to stimulate the economy would be substantial retraining of displaced workers without the skills needed by the new economy and stuck in the new structural unemployment (as I call it).

Mass deportation of undocumented workers will also cause a labor shortage and push unemployment higher. Most Americans do not want to work at low paying arduous labor jobs.

--Some USA Infrastructure Planned Projects-but not funded.

--Port of New Orleans--$1.2 billion, deepen port to allow larger ships

--Jasper Ocean Terminal--$4.5 billion, provide access for large container ships to Port of Savannah, Georgia

--Texas Central Railroad--$10 billion, high speed passenger rail Houston-Dallas, Texas. 50,000 weekly commuters

--Bay Delta Conservation Plan-$25 billion, 150 deep tunnels to carry water from Northern to Southern California

--Bus Rapid Transit in cities across USA--$5 billion, Chicago Pace, Streetcars Oklahoma City and Milwaukee

-Tappan Zee Hudson River 3-mile Bridge, New York--$4 billion, building now, mostly non-federal funds.

READERS NOTES: Why is updated good infrastructure important ?

Port of New Orleans expansion

Part-time workers considered as full time

The US Department of Labor also only counts as unemployed those who are still actively looking and have looked for a job within the past 30 days. If you stopped looking for over 30 days but would still like a job you are not counted as unemployed nor as part of the work force, you disappear, and are considered a discouraged worker, currently 600,000 are in that category. Then there is a larger group that has given up looking for over a year and are now also not counted and are now not considered part of the labor force. That is about 6 million people that have vanished into the underground economy, working independently for cash or barter, usually for less income with no medical benefits provided, and therefore no taxes paid to support the government budget, and with simpler lifestyles. Some of these are early retirees, about 2 million, so maybe they are ok, unless their social security benefit is low. Without extended Medicaid or Obamacare health subsidies none of them would have healthcare. This also means lower GDP growth rates (Hello Donald Trump-4% or bust!). This category is about 3% of the labor force. Another 5 million people are working part-time but looking for full time. Yes folks, our government counts part time as employed so if you lose a $60,000 job, and pick up a $20,000 job, you are still considered employed. Add all this up and you get an unemployment rate of 10%, more realistic, then 3.4%. And I think the Department of Labor undercounts. They telephone 60,000 people a month and ask a series of questions. Really! I call all of this the New Structural Unemployment. This is a long-term trend that is a drag or anchor on robust economic growth. Most likely a 3% GDP economic growth rate will be difficult to obtain and sustain. Could this be the "New Normal". Did you know the entire textile industry in South Carolina was wiped out, 100,000 high paying union factory jobs which effected entire cities were moved to China and other small Asian and South American countries? Massive textile mills closed (Canon Mills-towels). And they are not coming back. These people, many who are over 50 years, need retraining. They were not left with huge lifelong pensions and severance packages like high level executives. They also are stuck in South Carolina close to their families and roots. You just can't pick up and move if you have no money. This is permanent new structural unemployment, or underemployment, or low wage, or just plain stuck in a bad economic place. Ain't your fault. I met Steve this summer at my apartment complex pool, he is very tan. He hangs out there from 3-5 PM, relaxing and using his cell phone trying to get Social Security and Medicare and a job. He is concerned and discouraged. His Social Security benefit will be low, $750, because he never had any high paying jobs, although he is a sociology major and graduate of the University of Wisconsin. Since he had a broken back some years ago his ability to work is very limited and disability was not available because it was declined although he suffers from back pain. He now is going on Social Security. His savings are close to gone which he has been using to supplement his income so what he will do to survive? Now he can quality for some Section 8 housing assistance (but you still may have to pay up to 30% of your income) and a small food allowance of $200 per month and $3 meals at the senior center and some free dinners at churches and charity. Yes, he has a delicate lifeline, but precarious and he is anxious, no way to live your senior years. With his back problem few jobs are available. Ok, he might get by for another 20 years with a barebones budget. A problem is since our Congress has severely underfunded housing assistance here in Albuquerque there is at least a one year waiting period. In Tucson AZ. 27,000 people are on a waiting list. Thank goodness with a combined Medicare and Medicaid his medical expenses are low. And Congress is trying to limit Medicaid benefits. Some countries are worse, but this is the wealthiest country in the world (and the largest military). He still needs to earn $500 per month to make ends meet at an advanced age.

The strange good news is that the total population is going sideways and will be decreasing soon (and the white population is already decreasing) requiring less job competition and public services. The US Birth Fertility Rate is about breakeven (2.0) meaning as many people are being born as are dying. And the white fertility rate is 1.7, so us American white people will be gone later this century! The typical American white family used to have 3-6 children back in the 1950's. In Europe, Russia, China, and Japan this rate is 1.2-1.8, meaning some countries and races will disappear this century! Except Immigration is keeping those rates barely above breakeven. The USA is 322 million people. Without immigration since 1975 the population would only be about 280 million, and much more racially white. Walmart's sales would be much lower. The US economy and resources would be much less, so be careful when you want to limit immigration or have less children of any race, the country may vanish! Who needs enemies when we may be gone anyway! LOL. And if you don't like the French culture and attitudes, don't worry, someday it will become a middle eastern country.

 And oh yeah, I almost forgot, I have a pair of New Balance running shoes that were made in VIETNAM! $150.

GLOBALIZATION HEADWINDS & WAGE PRESSURE

Since 1992 almost two billion new people have entered the world labor pool as China, India, and the former Soviet Bloc of Eastern Europe opened their economies and trade barriers fell. This new large supply of labor has caused downward unrelenting pressure on wages.

Extensive new technology has replaced workers and also caused a need for more education. The US is falling behind here. Various educational rating agencies have placed the US back into the upper teens, the Asian countries are way out in front with western European countries next. Three million American highly skilled job openings are currently available. Corporations are lowering standards to fill these positions. In higher education the USA is near the top. Great research universities.

Digital and internet communication has enabled the world to easily and for very low cost communicate. Since 1946 trade restricting tariffs have almost been eliminated encouraging foreign trade.

Very low interest rates have shifted investment into tangible assets like stocks, bonds, real estate, and corporate purchases of other firms with this cheap money which has mostly benefited the wealthy and corporate entities.

The huge reduction in labor unions has restricted labor wage bargaining power.

If more voters understood these factors, they would be less likely to follow leaders who promised they could solve economic problems by themselves by the force of their personality and business skills. Sound familiar President Trump supporters? High tariffs are bad for the economy and a tax on people.

After much reflection I think I have drifted into being a quasi-socialist who believes in economic freedom, choice, and free markets somewhat like France, Sweden, and Germany. I also consider myself to be both a liberal and a conservative (small caps). Liberal because I believe in the liberal values that founded this country; freedom, democracy, building a strong fair-minded country. And conservative because I want to conserve our resources. The land, wildlife, soldiers, national wealth and financial reserves, people's welfare, health, educational system. Done with careful planning that assesses the risks of policies-go slowly and minimize risk. The far-Right policies are radical, and also the far Left. That is high risk-taking policies which has can have dangerous outcomes. Start a war in Iraq and ISIS pops up. Have anti-Russian policies and Russia retaliates. Cut back medical benefits and the population gets sicker and the economy weaker. Have huge tax cuts and huge budget deficits occur which destabilize the USA and impair our credit rating and capability to borrow to fund our country. If increased economic growth does not occur which is fairly likely based on current trends, and the economy falls back into a recession then unemployment shoots up. Cut too many domestic programs quickly and the people are harmed. I would say if tax rates are sharply increased as some on the far left have advocated, that is risky radical policy, which could financially destabilize the USA. Go slow and carefully and stay the course. Change when new circumstances dictate gradually and predictably.

I tell my students entrenched ideology kills or is harmful. Avoid it.

Blend of socialism and capitalism

So this model of a blend of socialism and capitalism I advocate emphasizes average people and a managed free market capitalistic economic system (that does not suffocate the economy with too much regulation and red tape). At age 72 it is liberating and exciting to share my ideas with you even if you disagree. The USA needs help, guidance, a philosophy, a plan. Will the real USA please stand up? Sweden is a highly socialist country and has an economic growth rate of 2.4%, over twice that of the European Union. The USA has been stuck at 2%, with a recent increase to 3%, but will it last? Is it sustainable? And guess what? Since WW II there have been 6 Democrat and 6 Republican Presidents with Democrats in power for 33 years and Republicans for 36 years. During Republican Administrations the growth rate has been 2.7% and during Democratic Presidents 4.2%. And the democrats are those liberals with big government policies that are accused of slowing down the economy? I don't think so. And most major wars occur under Democratic administrations.

Note: President Trumps' Republican tax plan is very risky. It creates huge budget deficits, higher interest rates, increased income inequality, and is based on a highly speculative increase in GDP growth of 3-5%, way above the current 2% trendline, which may be the "new normal". From 1946 to 1974 the US economy grew at a 3.5% growth rate when all conditions for the US were favorable. There were not the entrenched economic "drag" effects of Globalization, slow labor productivity, slow population growth (no more baby boomers), and increased use of technology to replace workers. The US Steel plant in Gary, Indiana produces the same amount of steel now with 1/6 of the workforce than in 1970. If this high GDP growth does not materialize then the economy will crash and burn with much higher unemployment. The high government "Fiscal Stimulus" of the economy began in January (2018) is coming at a bad time with a fairly strong economy and low unemployment which can ignite high inflation. The economy can also fade within 18 months.

UPDATE US ECONOMY MAY 2019

The Dow-Jones Industrial Average seems to have topped out at around 26,000. Unemployment is a very low at 3.4%. Alan Greenspan, former Federal Reserve Chairman, has stated the is the tightest labor market he has ever seen. However, this does not take into account the high number of people working part-time at low wages and the high number of discouraged workers and those who have dropped out of the labor force. The economy is undergoing a strong fiscal stimulus due to the large individual and corporate tax cuts and increase in defense spending. This is causing a very large US budget deficit that will exceed 1 trillion dollars, almost double the deficit before the recent tax bill. In turn this is putting pressure for higher US interest rates and a strong dollar which will tend to slow the US economy. Reduced federal regulation of business is probably also contributing to a stronger economy. However, one needs to be wary of negative spill-over effects like too much financial risk taking or environmental degradation. Concern about future inflation is causing the Federal Reserve to aggressively tighten money. Inflation and wage growth still remain low due to the effects of Globalization and jobs in lower wage industries and more short-term contract workers. Amazon has just raised its minimum wage to $15 per hour and Walmart to $11. This seems due to political pressure but might be the beginning of a trend to higher wages and higher inflation. Future earnings of large High-Tech companies are being reduced. Housing is showing signs of weakness. Automobile sales and manufacturing are starting to diminish. There is now some talk of a recession in 2020.

Oh, and what happened to the campaign promises of paid maternity leave and a massive infrastructure program? They would improve the population well-being and boost the economy.

GINI RATIOS of Various Countries.

The Gini Ratio measures the degree of income and <u>wealth inequality in a country</u>. The higher the ratio, the higher the level of wealth concentration at the top. NOTE: In Scandinavia the idea of "economic" equality is considered a moral value and embedded in the culture.

GINI RATIOS

South Africa—70%

Zambia—62%

Brazil—50%

Mexico—48%

Chile—47% (down from 57% 1990)

Philippines—46%

USA—44%

Russia—42%

China—42%

Venezuela—39% (47% in 2010)—Socialist Restructuring

Vietnam—35%

Iran—35% (down from 42% 2007)

Poland, Canada, Germany 32%

France—29%

Sweden, Finland—25%

Prior to 1965 the US poverty rate was consistently 22%. After President Lyndon Johnson's Great Society programs were passed into law in the 1960's, called "The War on Poverty" the US poverty rate declined by ½ to 11% and stayed there for several decades. It gradually rose to 13%' dropped to 11% in the prosperous 1990's, and rose to 12% until 2009, when it jumped to 19% during the Great Recession and has fallen to 15% now. Without the social safety net the poverty rate would be 29%. The programs passed then are essentially the social safety net today. None of them would be passed by the US Congress today. These are Medicaid, Medicare, expansion of Social Security, Food Stamps, Housing assistance and public housing, funding for mass transit, model cities, slum housing and deteriorated neighborhood clearance, the Elementary and Secondary Education Act providing hot school lunches and breakfasts, textbooks, special education programs for ALL income levels, Operation Head Start providing early childhood education, the Higher Education Act providing low cost large funding of student loans and Pell grants, scholarships, The National Foundation for the Arts, Corporation for Public Broadcasting, Amtrak Rail. Also the Job Corp., Vista, Peace Corp. (all dedicated to rebuilding national and worldwide distressed areas), and the Appalachian Redevelopment Act providing highways, clean water, health centers for Appalachia. And many of the environmental programs/laws were started, Clean Water, Wilderness Preservation, Clean Air Act. Also the National Highway and Vehicle Safety Act, Department of Transportation, Truth in Packaging Act.

This is when the major civil rights laws were created that substantially gave African-American Black people enforceable rights that prevented racial discrimination.

The 24th Amendment abolished the Poll Tax. Yes in southern states one had to pay a fee to vote which eliminated poverty-stricken Blacks from voting. The Voting Rights Act abolished literacy tests for voting and permitted Federal monitoring of Federal elections to prevent local restrictions from interfering with voting. A US Supreme Court ruling recently weakened the Voting Act.

These programs brought the senior citizens poverty rate from 28% to 10%. Before Medicaid and Medicare 50% of senior citizens had no health care insurance and many could not afford to pay cash. Of course people didn't live as long in 1960. And today 2/3's of seniors use Medicaid to pay for assisted living and nursing homes. That will be me as well. And you?? All of these programs were approved by Congress from 1964-1970.

When I grew up we split our modest house in half, with my grandparents in front, and me and my parents in the back. We each had our own small kitchen, living room, and bedroom, and shared a bathroom. Most homes had what was called a mother- in-law small apartment for the aging grandparents.

In Western Europe countries like France, Germany, Sweden, United Kingdom-England have poverty rates in the 6%-9% range but without a safety net poverty would be 28%, just like the USA. These countries have higher benefits and of course higher taxes.

Here in Albuquerque there is a different kind of quaint park, with large trees, green grass, a little hilly, picnic tables, frisbee golf, and a long paved walking path. Families use this for picnics on holidays, there are many walkers. I run there, and my school had a picnic there. It is named Roosevelt Park after our depression era president FDR. A plaque is there, stating this park was built by the Workers Progress Administration in 1935, a depression era employment federal program. Millions of men went through these programs to rebuild America, and help people live. The average man put on 12 pounds, had housing and recreation. Most of the small salary was sent home to their families. Guess what, this was a socialistic program. It helped save America from a revolt and destitution. Today the public benefits of this park continue to people who never lived then. This is a great example of public benefits provided by good government funding. Economists call this a positive externality.

GREAT DEPRESSION 1935 UNEMPLOYED OVER 25%. Public government employment massive programs probably prevented national riots and saved Capitalism while preventing Socialism in the USA.

READERS NOTES

Define Socialism. Is it a good idea? Why?

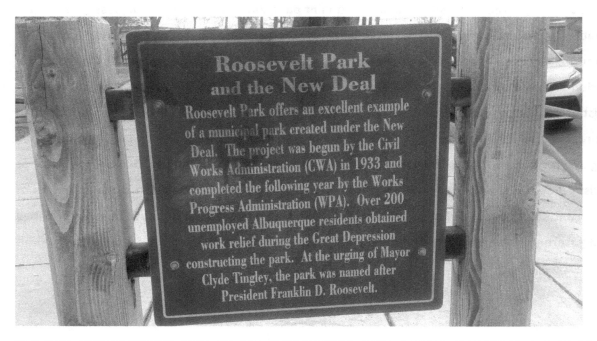

BUILT IN ALBUQUERQUE 1935 BY 200 UNEMPLOYED MEN. WORKS PROGRESS ADMINISTRATION NATIONAL PROGRAM. THE PARK IS STILL USED TODAY 83 YARS LATER. IT HAS PROVIED MUCH PUBLIC BNEFITS.

LUNCH TIME CCC or CIVILIAN CONSERVTION CORP. These 200 men did national soil, road, and forest restoration. Millions of trees were planted. The current National Park lodges were built. This is an example of tremendous public national benefits lasting until this day.

Conclusion: Countries that have higher government spending on public projects in the economy have less income inequality.

HUEY LONG-Governor of Louisiana 1933-35

See his speech on UTUBE "Everyman a King". He was quite a character and a socialist who believed that wealthy people had to have less wealth and income and redistribute it to the average man and woman. He thought Franklin Roosevelt did not go far enough and was too conservative. The moderate income people in Louisiana loved him. It is incredible that this red very conservative state today could have been so liberal in 1933. But Louisiana has always been isolated and under the influence of French culture and attitudes, different from the rest of the USA. In his speech he provides homespun examples and he oversimplifies the solutions to the inequities of capitalism. But you get the point and it is amusing to hear him with his deep southern accent and phrases. He was considered a possible presidential candidate. He was assassinated in 1936.

SOME WOW STUFF ABOUT THE USA AND ITS ECONOMY

Firstly, The US Stock Market-Dow Jones Industrial Average-Corporate America

The growth in the US stock market averages since 1980 is amazing!!

Since 1900 the compounded rate of return for the DJIA is 9.6%. This is through numerous national crises, wars, recessions.

In 1980 the Dow Jones Average was at 1,000, a long term peak at that time. In 2018, thirty-eight years later it is 25,000. A 25x increase or 2,500%. Net of the inflation rate or adjusted for the consumer price index plus dividends of 3% per year is a compounded yearly return of 9%. During this time there was much uncertainty. Real Market Returns per year: 1980-2000 -- 12%; 2000-2017-- 5%; 2012-2017 -- 14%. The increase is the consequence of American corporations increasing earnings through innovation, efficiencies, and staying competitive worldwide. It is also the result of long-term political stability and confidence in America's future worldwide. I think amid all the negativism and chaos in the media we forget this fact. All these earnings have produced prosperity and taxes to support the government public sector, the military, and national security. Of course low wages have also helped.

Second, the gigantic growth and innovation of the American High-Tech corporations. Amazon in 20 years is now the largest corporation in the world, just ahead of Apple. And it has revolutionized the way we shop. Think of Amazon, Google (Alphabet), Microsoft, Facebook, Tweeter, Netflix, the world wide Web-Internet, digital phones. I have Facebook friends around the world and can call anyone anywhere in an instant. This is just incredible and seems like the Eighth Wonder of The World. On August 2, 2018 Apple's market capitalization reached 1 trillion dollars, remarkable. And the top 5 high-tech companies in size are equal to 40% of the total capitalization of the entire NASDAQ! Talk about market power and influence.

Third, the US legal and court system. It is reliable and transparent. It protects the rights of people, business owners, corporations, and governments, and allows for the peaceful solution of conflicts. Lawyers know the rules to steer their clients out of trouble. The US economy could not function without this legal order. This is not true in many countries.

Fourth, the entertainment and movie industry, HOLLYWOOD!!

The amount of mass media produced is just mind boggling. All kinds of films, videos, television, worldwide sporting events you name it. Outstanding actors, producers, directors. And think of all those other support workers you see at a movie, the credits, all who worked on the movie, just incredible that so many people are employed. And so many unheard of actors too. Agents making deals for stars, for newcomers, for all the writers. Distribution is worldwide, and series are syndicated and shown on TV stations for many years after initial distribution. And enormous sums of money are made by the stars. They live in lavish homes, receive world recognition, and are guests on talk shows. In 2017 box office receipts worldwide were $40 billion. That is just people walking into movie theaters. The entire US movie and entertainment industry had receipts of $703 billion in 2017. Home video alone was $108 billion. The filmed entertainment sector had a trade surplus of $13 billion, a real boost to the US economy. Visit Los Angeles California, USA and see and feel it for yourself.

And what we do without filmed sports and Major League Baseball and NFL professional football. Life would be so boring for many people.

US Department of Defense World Headquarters Pentagon

<u>**Fifth, and of course,**</u> <u>the gigantic US military and their headquarters building, the PENTAGON.</u> To me it is a unique World Wonder. It is 5 sided with 5 floors with a large open area common in the middle. Probably a few underground floors too. It is 6.6 million square feet with 17.5 miles of corridors. 26,000 people work there. It is the world's largest building by floor area. The CIA headquarters is not far away. I have been in the Pentagon several times and waked through it. You can easily get lost. Military personnel, mostly higher-ranking officers and NCO's, are busily walking about, dressed in everyday casual uniforms or some in desert combat fatigues and combat boots. All doing office work. You see and feel the power here. I was there on a tour in 2016 and we walked 1 mile inside and didn't even realize it! There are long huge hallways, some are off limits. From here the US effectively influences much of the world. The organization and management of this world-wide high tech $700 billion military network is incredible.

In 1947 President Truman instituted the Truman Doctrine foreign policy and increased the size and scope of the US CIA (Central Intelligence Agency) in response to the expansion of the Soviet Union's new power. It reoriented U.S. foreign away from its stance of withdrawal from regional conflicts not directly involving the U.S., to one of possible intervention in faraway conflicts. It became the policy of the US to support free peoples who are resisting attempted subjugation by armed minorities or by outside pressures. Thus began a new policy of defending democratic nations when in the best interest of the United States. But the US also supported the status quo, harsh autocratic regimes that supported US interests but suppressed most of their population. This policy has harmed people in many countries and justified armed interventions, and the hawkish current foreign policy strategy of the Deep State and Neocons. Frankly all of Congress too. This way of thinking must end and an appropriately sized and organized military that complements a thoughtful foreign policy is needed.

Veterans and Armistice Day November 11, 2018. Free meals at Applebee's and Golden Corral. Thank you. For some reason I always choke up when someone thanks me for my service. Although I am somewhat of a political rogue, I am proud of having served in the US Army. I believe that gives me extra credibility when being critical of US Foreign Policy. Too many bold loud talking "Hawks" have never served. I view them with skepticism.

The new US defense budget includes a $13 BILLION new aircraft carrier. The US now has 11, China 1, Russia 1. This is unnecessary and an example of bloated military budgets and over strength. Money needs to be used for domestic programs.

Today November 6, 2018 is the <u>mid-term election in the USA</u>. The turnout is ENORMOUS as people flock to the polls to vote for opposing parties but more importantly, opposing attitudes about government and leadership and the future of the country's direction. This is the ultimate check on "government" and power, the people still determine major outcomes, they are the ultimate power. This is what is great about America despite all its current shortcomings. Foreign governments (and people within the influential USA power structure) would be well advised to remember the right of the people to determine their future and a free press. The ultimate power.

ME GIVING A BRIEFING ON RUSSIAN FOREIGN POLICY IN PENTAGON! (on a visitor's tour)

And so the Pentagon grew and grew in size as the role of the military increased. If you criticize US foreign policy and the military, you might be deemed unpatriotic by much of the American people. The US may have been militarized, little by little. People everywhere congratulate soldiers for their service. That is fine. But what about other type of service, like me working as a teacher on remote Indian Reservations? Or social workers in dangerous urban areas? Or care givers to the elderly? And let's not forget about the United States Senate, wise level-headed people working together looking at the big picture of the future and well-being of the USA.

I still think one has to keep in mind the US has the highest overall quality of life compared to Russia and China. It is mostly safe, sanitary, good health care, decent education, roomy available housing, plentiful consumer goods, cars, and reliable. And mostly free. The world still sees the US as "Good Guys".

WALKING AROUND ECONOMICS---An Interesting Story---In November 1981 I was working for Greyhound Leasing and Financial Corp., a new job. I went on a business trip to drum up some business in Peoria, Illinois, an industrial town of 120,00 people. About 6 in the evening I was sitting at the busy hotel bar and struck up a conversation with a man sitting next to me, who was a marketing manager for the gigantic Caterpillar Tractor Corporation headquartered in Peoria. They are the #1 construction company in the world, their equipment is painted all yellow. I'm sure you have seen it. The economy was really starting to fade, as the Federal Reserve was beginning to substantially raise interest rates to stem high inflation. I'll always remember what he said. "Don't tell anybody this, but we have NO worldwide backlog (of sales)". Wow, a disaster as this company's sales outlook was and is a reliable predictor of business conditions. And sure enough in 1982 the economy collapsed and capital spending just about went to zero. Our equipment leasing business went down 70% as short-term interest rates soared to 20% (usually 4%-8%). I will never forget this. This is an example of what I tell my students is walking around economics. No need to have a PhD in economics. Just look around and listen. In 2003 I was just amazed at the new home construction in the Chicago area. Never seen anything like it! Home prices were rising at a rate 2-3 times the historical average. And then a friend went to work for a mortgage company and credit approval criteria was almost non-existent. Hardly any documentation for people with moderate to low incomes to buy a $200,000-$500,000 house. I knew something big was occurring. And sure enough, in 2008 the world economy and the housing market and financial/banking industry collapsed. When something doesn't seem right, it isn't.

READERS NOTES:

Should the US stop the harmful embargo/sanctions against Cuba and recognize it as a friendly state. And provide some money for their consumer economy to improve? What about Venezuela? Is it an enemy or threat to USA? Why or why not?

HAVANNA CUBA-GREAT MEDICAL AND ECOLOGICAL-VERY LOW CONSUMER GOODS

CUBA

CUBA AND VENEZUELA—

The situation in Venezuela is in flux, chaotic, and experiencing intervention from several large countries. The socialist government is under duress and extreme pressure to disband and allow the political opposition forces to assume the government under the direction of the United States. The economy has crashed as the government overspent on necessary social and infrastructure for the masses of poor people. The budget deficit soared to 30% of GDP causing widespread inflation, reducing the purchasing power of people's income. Government price controls on consume goods just caused huge shortages and civilian unrest. The attempt to dislodge the current government by the US implementing severe economic sanctions has only made the suffering and shortages worse. The large decline in the price of oil by almost 50% drastically reduced essential government revenues. Venezuela imported 90% of their consumer and capital goods, so this left the government starving for revenue. The currency crashed and lost its purchasing power and ability to accommodate foreign trade.

I do not see why US policy towards these countries should be so harsh. I have thought that if the USA is an exceptional and helpful nation then why not give both Cuba and Venezuela $250 billion in economic assistance, humanitarian aid, food, and technical assistance instead of clamoring for $ 1 trillion dollars for lethal military weapons and aid to Ukraine? Why is the USA always so concerned about small countries that are not so friendly to US ideas and interests? And with Cuba, a shameful 55-year punitive embargo even after the fall of the Soviet Union in 1992 when Russia turned capitalist and was no longer a threat from an alliance with Cuba? The United Nations General Assembly has passed a resolution to end the embargo signed by over 100 countries. Only the US and Israel refused to sign. Maybe a socialist economy (with some elements of democracy) would have worked better with US cooperation. These countries enemies, a threat? C'mon, get serious. Both have had food shortages, inflation and also violence in Venezuela, and a loss of highly skilled technical educated workers. Do these countries have huge armies or are they undermining the USA? No way. Cuba has an excellent educational and medical system providing free health care for the entire population now since the Cuban Revolution in 1960. It also has a gold rating for environmental preservation. And yes, the consumer economy is lacking, not so good. So you see, the entire world has some socialistic characteristics including the USA. Countries can still cooperate with different political and economic systems.

The CIA has tried to assassinate Fidel Castro many times and has consistently attempted to undermine the Cuban government. That may be a reason the Cuban government has such a defensive harsh political climate. It is self-defense. You know the Revolution in 1960 overthrew the very corrupt and harsh Batista military authoritarian regime that did not provide benefits and basic needs for most of the people but supported US economic interests. The elite lived like Royalty and the small middle class prospered. The average person suffered, and democracy was not apparent. Yes, the wealthy and middle class fled and lost much property. That was unfortunate, but it was 55 years ago. And in 1960 Fidel Castro, trained as a lawyer, came to the USA and its banks for financial and friendly help to rebuild Cuba. But he was rejected and so turned to Russia for assistance. You see how things could have been different? No Cuban missile crisis would have occurred. A Latin American professor told me that Cubans who have emigrated to the USA miss the social solidarity and cultural community of socialist Cuba but like having a good job and money. With US help Cuba may have been a more open society and freer economy, and more prosperous.

Under the Hugo Chavez Venezuelan government vast social programs were done improving and providing free medical care, schooling, housing for the large impoverished population. The poverty rate dropped from 56% to 28%, in line with other South American countries. Common wisdom in the news today is that Venezuela was the most prosperous nation in South America until 1998. But the country also had the highest poverty rate and most of the population suffered from terrible living conditions. The wealth did not trickle down. Now the country poverty rate is again climbing with food shortages and high inflation. Too much of this was financed by borrowing and increasing inflationary spending. The reduction in the world price of oil by 50% and the loss of oil company professionals worsened the economy. Venezuela nationalized US oil companies which does not create friends. Too much change too soon with too few resources and we get a disorganized economy, now in chaos. But still let Cuba and Venezuela find their own way with US and Latin American support, a blend of socialism and market freedom with economic growth. Different but not in opposition to the USA political and economic model. Nationalizing the foreign oil companies was a bad idea. A better choice would have been for the government to negotiate higher oil royalties and require the oil companies to hire and train more Venezuelan people. And also to reduce the amount of complex new government business regulation and high taxes. Venezuela tried to do too much too quickly.

The major oil companies have not suffered since their Venezuelan oil operations were nationalized, as that worldwide risk is already built into their costs and profit plan with few benefits to the general population. The Venezuelan government owns Citgo, a large American oil company, that has pledged 49% of its equity to Russia as collateral for a loan. So be careful USA. Perhaps a compromise could be reached in which Venezuela repays a portion of the oil companies lost property over 50 years, in return for technical assistance to make their oil operations efficient and updated. This would stabilize the country.

OLD GLORY USA FLAG

American Exceptionalism

I dislike using this phrase because it implies America is better and has a moral right and obligation to intervene in other countries and world affairs to spread its economic model and political system. Many people around the world resent this attitude. It leads to bad policy, like invading Iraq. The USA should not consider itself as necessarily better but having excellent characteristics and some not so favorable that unfortunately have tended to cause harmful unintended consequences. It also has political myths that never really existed. Yes, it is terrific to have dreams and aspirations for a better world.

But isn't Germany exceptional with a strong economy and a highly skilled workforce; Sweden with a good economy and excellent social benefits; France with worker job security and a beautiful culture and city, Paris; Norway with a humane and reformative prison system; Finland with an outstanding progressive educational system; China with marvelous new cities and a thriving economy; the United Kingdom with an excellent parliamentary form of democratic government and tradition; and Russia with the stunningly beautiful elaborate subway system, a highly educated population, and the Kremlin; and Iran or ancient Persia with a thriving civilized culture going back over 2000 years??

Your thoughts:

I am not encouraging a naive disengagement from the world, but rather an integrated approach with a changed attitude, a modified presentation.

Me in Capitol at statue of Hawaiian Chief

MY ECONMIC SOCIAL AND POLITICAL PHILOSOPHY:

"PROSPERITY WITH FAIRNESS"

YOU ARE NOT ENTITLED TO EVERYTHING YOU HAVE GOTTEN IN AMERICA REGARDLESS OF_____(you fill in your rationale.)

WE SHARE THE ENTIRE PIE

UPLIFTING BUILDS STRENGTH

YOU CANNOT EXIST IN A VACUMN

OUTCOMES ARE NEGOTIATED

STRUGGLE IS NORMAL----ACCEPTANCE IS NOT

EACH CITIZEN HAS A CONSTITUTIONAL RIGHT TO:

AFFORDABLE QUALITY HEALTH CARE

GOOD EDUCATION

DECENT AFFORDABLE HOUSING

ADEQUATE ECONOMIC AND SOCIAL SAFETY NET FOR MODEST INCOME AND LESS FORTUNATE. THIS EXTENDS BEYOND THE OFFICIAL POVERTY LEVEL AND INCLUDES MANY SENIOR CITIZENS

* There is a DUTY for everyone to pay for this Society

* Government Service is a duty and an honor (both civil and military)

* Public investment in people and physical structures is necessary to build the Infrastructure for a thriving private economy

* We need a safe and healthy environment-consideration for "jobs" is important but sometimes secondary

* *I too am a "conservative". I believe in conserving people, natural resources, wildlife, national government and individual financial wealth, our soldiers, and stable government. National Economic policies should provide long term sustainability.*

* I call it Social Capitalism—"Build wealth with a DUTY to support a HEALTHY AND HONORABLE SOCIETY"

SOCIAL JUSTICE------ECONOMIC FAIRNESS

Yes everybody this is it—think about it. Is this the USA today?

BROOKLYN BRIDGE INFRASTRUCTURE BUILT 1883-STILL PROVIDING TRANSPORTATION

SOCIAL SECURITY and MEDICARE (and what about DENTAL for Seniors)

THERE IS NO CRISIS!!

<u>Congress and Right Wing Think Tanks (or Propoganda Tanks). I fully funded myself during my lifetime of work and payroll taxes! I did some math.</u> My average income over a 25 year (1972-1997) career in banking was $50,000. 2.7% was deducted for Medicare (includes employer matching tax). That is $1500 PER YEAR. The Future Value of a $1500 annuity at 4% interest is $65,000. Since then 20 years have passed. At 3.5% interest this amount doubles to $130,000. So I have a $130,000 reserve to pay my health expenses. At 3% interest I cover $3900 health expenses per year about double of what Medicare Advantage has been paying since age 65. Since I got cancer that amount is about $5,000-$10,000 per year. My expected life span is 85, another 13 years. I will most likely never use it up. And we also pay a

$134 per month Medicare Premium (up from $106, a 27% increase in one year!) and large copays. Being admitted to a hospital will cost you about $450 per day for 5 days or $2250. And $300 for an MRI. There is little or no dental coverage nor eyecare benefits. I recently financed a $928 crown at 15% for 5 years. And that is cheap.

Social Security payroll tax is 12% including employer matching tax. At an average earned income subject to the tax of $35,000, $4,200 was withheld each year which comes out to a sum of 330,00*. This will cover my $20,000 per year benefit for my lifetime even if I live to 90. At 4% interest that lump sum reserve will be earning $12,120 per year and when I die $170,000 will still be available to pay for other people who have earned less ($20,000-$12000=$8,000 surplus per year). Congress and Conservative Special Interest Groups are misleading us Americans. You see Congress spent all our money so now they have to raise taxes and cut benefits!

So we Seniors are still paying 14.7% payroll taxes even though we are on benefits. Including my employers share, $12,000 has been paid over the past 5 years on my part time income of $15,000. That is $6,000 out of my pocket. And $6,000 out of an extremely tight community college budget. It is extremely inequitable, unfair, and punitive to us and employers, who are less likely to hire us as they have to pay their share of the payroll tax. Thanks to you Congress and our Presidents. I am indignant, are YOU? *An outrage to us Seniors.*

If the current $125,000 earnings cap on the Social Security tax was removed Social Security would show a surplus! Now there is no tax on higher incomes. A person with $800,000 income pays $7500 FICA or .09%, $400,000 in earnings pays $7500 in FICA, a 1.5% effective rate. Someone at $125,000 pays $7500 and at a $30,000 income pays $1800. Both pay 6%. Not fair. It is a regressive tax. And yes, this is socialism, as the wealthy would be paying more for the same maximum benefit allowed, which is about $25,000 per year. It is income redistribution. I approve of this message (idea).

*Future value of an annuity at 3.5% over 25 years is a factor of 39. 39 x $4,200 = $163,800. From 1997-2017 is 20 years. The future value of $163,800 for 20 years at 3.5% compounded annually is $330,000.

READERS NOTES:

WHAT DO YOU THINK ABOUT HEALTH CARE IN THE USA?

OTHER REFLECTIONS

Jackson Park in Chicago next to Lake Michigan

MY EDUCATION:

I also have to mention that my education was superb. I was able to go to Northwestern University, a very prestigious and expensive private school that's in the Big Ten in Evanston, Illinois, on a track scholarship. Everything was paid for: room, board, tuition and books. Today that is over $65,000 per year! I was a kid from the South Side, could never have gotten in there, not enough money. But I did have the grades and the background to get admitted. I majored in history, got an A average in it. I loved it. Also, economics and political science. And that's when I developed my interests in international relations, the world, and national economic policies. At the age of 19, 20, it just hit me. And my politics and these interests haven't changed much since. I was awarded the Big 10 Medal of Honor and inducted into the Northwestern Athletic Hall of Fame.

Then I went on to get a Masters Degree in Business and Finance from the University of Chicago Graduate School of Business, something I am very proud.

University of Chicago The Midway Pleasance

JANUARY, 2016-AN INTERESTING TRIP TO WASHINGTON D.C-Russia again

My friend Merrillyn and I had dinner New Year's Eve 2015 at the popular Russia House restaurant in Washington DC. We were in town to look at all the monuments, museums, talk to people, and get an idea of attitudes there about foreign policy. About 12:30 AM I went outside where many people were gathered and met two young men, both Danish World Bank Executives. When I mentioned I had some socialist ideas they were shocked that I, a University of Chicago Graduate School of Business graduate, could have such ideas from a school with a strong free market capitalistic reputation. But life is not so simple. They also were shocked that I could have some favorable consideration for the Russian foreign policy point of view. They considered the USA the last outpost of a strong dynamic economy (unlike socialist Europe). Also, the only defender of Europe against the encroachment and influence of Russia. They certainly weren't comfortable going it alone. I found this interesting and surprising.

 During the trip I met a Russian scholar in the hotel and spent three nights discussing Russian history and current issues. The funny thing he was going to introduce me to a Russian cultural/political attaché to discuss Ukraine and my idea of teaching economics in Russia for 3 months. It didn't happen. The day before I left I went to the Russian Embassy compound to see it from the outside just out of curiosity. It looks like a small modern version of the Kremlin. In my silly casual way I was snapping pictures of the gigantic wall and several buildings, waving at cameras, and wandering outside. I did see the Russian Ambassador Kislyak arrive in the front gate in his new white BMW. Everyone there had one. And then a young US soldier I had just met on the bus on leave from CentCom HQ in Germany implied the US had many more than 89 secret small outposts around the world, mostly Special Forces. How Interesting.

Blurry image of Russian Embassy sign at entrance

Russian Embassy Compound-Huge

READERS NOTES:
DO YOU THINK RUSSIA AND THE USA WILL GET INTO MILITARY CONFLICT? HOW? WHERE?

NATIONAL USA LEADERS

James Lovell-Astronaut Apollo 13

In 1999 I drove a limousine in Chicago. I made many airport trips. It was a break after years of a high pressure banking/financial career. I liked it. And guess what? One time driving a passenger I noticed in the back seat was James Lovell going to visit his son in Lake Forest, Illinois. Wow! He was laconic, stoically quiet. I remember we were stuck at a long complex stoplight intersection of several roads. I watched him in the rearview mirror studying the traffic. He said "those stoplights need a reconfiguration". Here was an example of his engineering mind working away to solve a complex problem. I was impressed, and it certainly was indicative how an American hero steered the malfunctioning Apollo 13 spacecraft back to earth safely.

Martin Luther King Jr. and Malcolm X

Great brave African American leaders who advanced civil rights. I admire them. There is a community college in Chicago, named Malcolm X College.

Muhammad Ali

A great boxer who introduced a new way of fighting, very graceful, powerful, with a deliberate strategy in the ring. His resistance to the Vietnam war and refusal to be drafted into the US Army showed courage and sacrifice. He was barred from boxing for three years." I ain't fighting in no war to kill other brown people when my real enemy is racism here"

The Kennedy Family

President John F Kennedy inspired me as he ushered in a new time of national service and US pride. Humorous and insightful, he led America towards a bright future. At one time after graduation from college, I considered joining the Peace Corp and a career in government service. The entire family is amazing with 100 members today, many active in politics and other leadership positions. I think they combine compassion for all people, are "liberal", fair minded, realistic, well educated, and committed to their beliefs. And coming from extreme wealth! I can only hope one of them arises into a major charismatic inspirational national leader. I think the Russia problem could be resolved realistically and peacefully and bridge the widening gap with that country. It needs to be done soon.

CENTRAL NEW MEXICO COMMUNITY COLLEGE OR CNM

I put this section in here because the college has been so good to me. Teaching economics has been one of the greatest experiences of my life and my favorite job. I love reading about the world economy and conveying that to my students who are mostly from modest socioeconomic backgrounds. Their eyes are opened to new realities and perspectives. Teaching is a respected honorable profession and I am grateful to be part of it. You should be so lucky. Sadly, large enrollment declines are reducing classes and forcing me to consider other employment options.

READERS NOTES:

I think current and prior college students should receive a federal subsidy and a loan reduction based on income thresholds. Repayment terms need to be lengthened to 15 years at a low interest rate about 3%. But education should not be free for all. Already community college tuition is low and affordable. It is not unreasonable to expect students to graduate with some student debt. I admit student debt burdens overall are too high and tuition has become too high in relation to national income growth for the past 40 years. What is your opinion?

THANKS FOR READING MY BOOK

"If the United States continues looking for enemies it will cease to exist as a spiritually enlightened nation" [R. Schultz 2019]

THE FINAL PICTURE SECTION IS PERSONAL AND IS NOT PART OF THE BOOK TOPICS. I PUT IT HERE BECAUSE I WANT TO SHOW AVERAGE PEOPLE I AM JUST LIKE ONE OF THEM, AND ESPECIALLY FOR RUSSIANS. ALL OF US AMERICANS DO NOT SHARE THE ELITIST VIEWPOINTS THAT RUN THE UNITED STATES

.

PICTURE SECTION

At Pentagon Briefing Room giving presentation while on a to+ur

Me and Russian schoolchildren near Leningrad in 1968

The Russians Are Coming! Me in front of Russian Embassy, Imperial Russian Symbol lower left Russia House Restaurant Washington DC

Me, Sarah, John, Brooke, the Grandchildren

Family at Chicago Lakefront Blaine, Brooke, John, Sarah, Kate

Merrillyn, Family Friend

Me in official Los Angeles Dodgers baseball cap

My dogs in 2008 on Navajo Indian Reservation

My dogs, Starstream (above) and Snugly (below). The greatest Dachshunds I've ever known.

THIS PAGE INTENTIONALLY LEFT BLANK

Me after 3 mile walk run at local park route and the path, November 2, 2019

Below: Roosevelt Park, built 1933, still in use today, a great public work ; Central Park New York City. I ran in both parks, a real joy.

Me with wolf Forest in Albuquerque 2011 from Wolf Spirit Center

Malcolm, Carl, and me in 1955 South Side of Chicago 55th & Hermitage St.

WOLF SPIRIT-painted by Elton Three Stars-Oglala Lakota

Do you feel the spirit of the wolf looking inside you?

READERS NOTES: What do you know about wolves? And what do you think about them? I speak about the <u>wolves</u>. Pure ignorance and unconscionable cruelty by sports hunters and ranchers is killing large numbers. Wolves belong, they are social animals, never attacked a person unless in captivity and teased. My friend had two huge wolfdogs at home and I stood next to them in the kitchen. Just

gigantic, shoulders at my hips. I was very nervous and wary. Wolves Belong.

Above: Lakota Ceremonial Feather-Below Elton 3 Stars relaxing in my Lazy Boy chair. He painted the pictures of the wolf and my 2 dogs in this book. They are lifelike, uncanny, you see and feel their souls, their essence.

PICTURE OF ME 2002 BLACK HILLS LONGHAIR

TATONKA 2500 POUNDS MALE BUFFALO

Below: Pine Ridge Indian Reservation